The Digital Mirror

Reflections on Self in an Online World

by

Dr. ant

The Digital Mirror: Reflections on Self in an Online World

Contents

Introduction

In a world where every swipe and click reverberates through the threads of human experience, we stand on the precipice of unprecedented digital transformation. Technology has woven into the very fabric of our daily lives, altering not just how we interact with each other, but also how we perceive ourselves and our place in the world. This book seeks to explore the multilayered effects of this digital evolution on human behavior, aiming to shed light on how we've arrived at this moment and what it means for our future selves.

The rapid pace of technological advancement has left us grappling with profound changes. Where once distance dictated the cadence of connection, now immediacy and connectivity reign supreme. Time zones have become irrelevant in the domain of instant messaging and video calls, and physical borders fade away in the expanse of the virtual realm. These changes compel us to reflect on what it means to be human in an era where technology mediates so many of our interactions.

The human psyche is remarkably adaptable. However, the challenges posed by our increasingly digital lives are unique and complex. We've embarked on a journey to understand how digital life influences our minds, impacting everything from identity and community to emotion and mental health. Are we merely witnessing a transformation, or are we, in fact, active participants in the creation of a new societal and mental landscape? Each chapter in this book aims to dissect and examine these questions, providing a roadmap for understanding the intricate web of technology's impact on our psyche.

Digital technology offers tremendous benefits—greater access to information, new forms of entertainment, and opportunities for connectedness that were once unimaginable. Yet, this same technology also creates new challenges and dilemmas. The dual-edged nature of technology forces us to weigh the promise of digital progress against the potential pitfalls it creates. This dichotomy is at the heart of our exploration, not to judge technology as inherently good or bad but to understand its nuanced impact on humanity.

The digital landscapes we navigate each day are vast and varied, evolving as swiftly as new technologies emerge. Our interactions have transformed from face-to-face conversations to engagements mediated by screens. We craft personas for ourselves online, balancing these digital identities with our real-world selves. As we acclimatize to this new normal, it's crucial to question how these shifts influence our relationships, emotions, and mental states.

Social media platforms have particularly revolutionized the way we engage with the world. They promise connection and immediate access but also introduce a constant undercurrent of comparison, validation, and desire for approval. The allure of likes and shares taps into deep-seated human needs for recognition and belonging. Yet, as we scroll through curated versions of life, we must also consider the emotional toll of this engagement and how it colors our perception of reality.

Privacy and digital security are now at the forefront of our collective consciousness. Our personal data fuels the digital economy, raising questions about consent, ownership, and surveillance. As we share more of ourselves online, intentionally or inadvertently, we must navigate the complex web of privacy concerns, weighing the benefits of sharing against potential risks.

The deluge of information we consume daily can lead to a phenomenon known as information overload, leaving us fatigued and overwhelmed. Balancing our need for information with the necessity of mental health requires intentional strategies for managing digital consumption and finding moments of quietude amidst the noise.

The psychological impacts of living in a digital age are far-reaching. Digital stressors, coupled with the pressures of maintaining our online presence, create new mental health challenges. Recognizing these challenges and developing coping mechanisms will be essential for sustaining psychological well-being in an increasingly connected world.

As digital technology becomes ever more entwined with our lives, dependency on technology emerges as a critical issue. Understanding the signs of technology addiction and recognizing the importance of digital balance can empower us to maintain control over our tech use rather than allowing it to control us.

Relationships, too, have been redefined by digital means. Virtual intimacy and online conflicts present new dynamics that require us to reassess how we connect with others. Navigating these novel terrains of relationships necessitates a deeper understanding of connection and communication in cyberspace.

With our feet planted firmly in a digital present, the future calls us to prepare the next generation for a tech-centric world. Educating for a digital future involves teaching not just digital literacy but also critical thinking, ethical considerations, and adaptability to ever-evolving technologies.

Ultimately, as we peer into the horizon of digital evolution, we are tasked with considering the future of the self in a saturated digital landscape. Predicting trends and embracing change will be paramount as we seek to adapt to technological transformations. Ethical considerations in digital spaces will guide us in promoting responsible digital behavior, ensuring that technology serves humanity's best interests.

By examining these themes, this book endeavors not just to inform but to inspire a thoughtful dialogue about the role technology plays in our lives. As we delve into the chapters that follow, may we gain deeper insight into the ways technology molds our minds and behaviors, propelling us to navigate the digital frontier with awareness, prudence, and hope.

Chapter 1: The New Normal

The digital age has swiftly reshaped the contours of our daily lives, creating a reality that was once the realm of science fiction. We're now immersed in an environment where our interactions, work, and even our perceptions of self are interwoven with technological advancements. This new landscape demands that we redefine what "normal" means; it's not just about adapting to change but thriving within it. As we navigate this digital world, we're encouraged to build bridges across virtual and physical realms, gaining insights and fostering a deeper understanding of how technology impacts our emotions and behaviors. This journey requires introspection and adaptability, urging us to embrace our roles as both purveyors and pioneers in an era defined by screens and streams, seamlessly blending innovation with human nature. The key to thriving in this "new normal" lies in embracing the fluidity of change, harnessing the power of connectivity, and thoughtfully integrating these technologies into the fabric of our lives.

Understanding Digital Landscapes

The digital landscape is a multifaceted realm that, much like the physical world, is continually evolving and reshaping how we interact, think, and live. The advent of the internet has initiated a seismic shift not just in technology, but in societal norms, cultural dynamics, and even in the essence of being human. As technology continues to integrate itself into the core of daily life, it invites us to ponder its pervasive influence on our psyche, our perceptions, and our values.

Consider the internet as a living, breathing ecosystem teeming with information, opportunities, and challenges. It's an arena where innovation meets human interaction, creating a complex web of experiences that can enrich lives or exacerbate existing woes. The digital world is not just a tool; it is an environment — one that shapes and is shaped by its inhabitants. Its boundaries are constantly tested, its possibilities endlessly explored. To understand this landscape is to acknowledge its transformative power and the profound ways it influences human behavior.

For many, the digital realm feels like a second skin — a place where life's mundane tasks become seamlessly integrated with technology. You check the weather forecast while sipping your morning coffee or send a quick message before heading to a meeting. But beyond these conveniences lies a deeper integration that alters the very fabric of our societal interactions and personal relationships. It's important to reflect on the ramifications of this omnipresence; not just what we gain in efficiency but what we might lose in human connection.

Within this landscape, digital literacy becomes as vital as the ability to read or write. As we weave through a world mirroring the rapid pace of technological advancement, understanding digital literacy is akin to mastering a new language. It involves more than just navigating software and hardware; it encompasses deciphering algorithms, engaging with content critically, and protecting one's privacy within the vast expanse of cyberspace.

The exponential growth of digital technologies has also brought about a democratization of voice. Social media platforms amplify voices that might have once gone unheard, fueling movements and generating conversations on a global scale. Yet, with this democratization comes the cacophony of misinformation — a whirlwind of opinions and false narratives that can obscure truth and sabotage trust. Navigating this digital noise with a critical eye is essential for preserving one's mental well-being and understanding of the world.

Moreover, digital landscapes have become the new canvas for identity exploration and expression. As much as our physical environment influences who we are, so too does the digital realm shape our identities. We craft and curate personas, often blurring the lines between authenticity and artifice. It's a space where self-exploration and self-presentation converge, revealing the multifaceted nature of human identity in unprecedented ways.

The notion of space and time in digital landscapes is intriguingly fluid. You can traverse continents in milliseconds through a video call or lose track of time while meandering through endless content streams. This ability to transcend physical limitations alters our perception of how we inhabit the world, introducing new dynamics in how we structure our days and prioritize our interactions.

While there is much to celebrate in the digital realm's potential, it is imperative to remain vigilant of its pitfalls. The anonymity that the internet provides can be a double-edged sword, safeguarding identities while also emboldening behavior that would be unacceptable in the tangible world. The ease with which information spreads encourages creativity and knowledge-sharing but also poses significant risks to privacy and personal security.

Indeed, as we continue to immerse ourselves in this digital panorama, we must reflect on the responsibilities that accompany it. Ethical considerations play a crucial role, challenging us to ponder the moral implications of our digital actions. As we design and participate in digital spaces, the impetus lies within us to encourage inclusivity, respect, and empathy. Building a conscious community in these virtual realms can ultimately strengthen our sense of global connectivity and shared humanity.

Understanding digital landscapes involves a harmonious blend of optimism and caution, exploration and restraint. It requires society to embrace change while critically assessing the enduring consequences on human behavior. As tech-savvy individuals, we stand at the forefront of this exploration, equipped with the tools and the curiosity necessary to navigate this new normal. We must continually strive for a balance that honors the humanity at the core of this digital revolution, ensuring that in our quest for progress, we do not lose sight of what fundamentally connects us all.

Changing Interactions in a Digital World

In the ever-evolving digital landscape, our interactions have transformed in ways that earlier generations could only have imagined. By understanding the dynamics that underpin these changes, we can better grasp how they shape our relationships, communication, and even our own identities. The shifts in how we connect, learn, and collaborate are monumental, signaling an era of unprecedented growth and challenges.

With the ubiquity of smartphones, tablets, and laptops, communication has been liberated from the confines of time and place. The asynchronous nature of digital interactions allows people to communicate across time zones and continents. Whereas once we relied on letters and landlines, today we zip messages across cyberspace in mere moments. The very fabric of human interaction has been rewoven, creating both intricate patterns of connection and loose threads of superficial exchange.

Digital interaction has democratized access to information. A curious mind can delve into subject matter that was previously locked behind the gates of academia or industry. This open access fosters an environment ripe for innovation and creativity. However, the sheer volume of available information requires a discerning eye to parse truth from misinformation. The role of a digital citizen involves not only consuming but also curating and sharing responsibly.

Yet, in these new terrains, there is an undeniable intimacy juxtaposed with detachment. Platforms designed for connection often result in users projecting curated versions of themselves, crafting narratives that may or may not align with reality. The irony is that while we're more connected than ever, there's an increased sense of isolation. People might find themselves in a room full of individuals engrossed in their screens, communicating with others elsewhere but not with those physically present.

Emotional nuances, once conveyed through facial expressions or vocal intonations, are often lost or misunderstood in text-based communication.

To bridge this gap, digital language has evolved with emoticons, GIFs, and memes. These tools attempt to add color and emotion to otherwise monochrome words, but they too can fall short of conveying true human sentiment.

As we navigate through virtual spaces, our communication styles have adapted to different platforms. Social media, forums, and messaging apps each demand their unique etiquettes and norms. Understanding these unwritten rules is critical, as a misstep can lead to misunderstandings or conflict. The pace at which these platforms evolve adds to this complexity, compelling users to remain agile and informed.

Furthermore, digital mediums have altered traditional hierarchies in professional settings. Remote work and collaboration tools have flattened organizational structures, decentralizing power dynamics. Teams worldwide collaborate in real-time, working across hierarchical, geographical, and cultural boundaries. With these changes come opportunities for more inclusive environments, yet they also present challenges in maintaining cohesion and trust.

In education, digital interaction is redefining learning methodologies. Online classrooms and virtual resources provide flexibility and individualized learning paths. Students can access vast repositories of knowledge, leveraging forums and streaming lectures to enhance their understanding. As this trend continues, the role of teachers and educators evolves from sole knowledge providers to facilitators and mentors, guiding students through this digital labyrinth.

One noteworthy aspect of digital life is its potential for empathy and understanding across diverse cultures and perspectives. Social platforms provide windows into lives and experiences different from our own. Engaging with these narratives can foster a greater sense of global empathy, encouraging solidarity and action for global causes. However, the echo chamber effect can just as quickly create division and misunderstanding if not navigated with care.

The rapid pace of digital interaction highlights the age-old tension between convenience and meaningful engagement. Instant gratification and broad networks compete with the depth and richness of traditional, face-to-face interactions. As we assimilate these new norms and tools into our daily lives, a balancing act emerges. The quality of our engagements, rather than their quantity, becomes the metric of digital success.

Despite its challenges, the digital era holds promise. It invites a reevaluation of what it means to connect deeply and authentically in an increasingly interconnected world. There is potential for unprecedented collaboration and shared experiences. Those who harness the power of digital communication with empathy and responsibility stand to create meaningful and lasting impacts both online and offline.

As we continue to explore these digital possibilities and adapt to evolving communication landscapes, understanding the essence of human connection becomes more crucial than ever. With intentionality, we can shape our interactions to enhance, rather than dilute, the human experience in this burgeoning digital age.

Chapter 2: The Online Persona

In our interconnected world, the concept of the online persona emerges as both a mirror and a mask of our true selves. As we navigate digital platforms, we're not just sharing updates or images; we're deliberately crafting narratives of who we are or aspire to be. This creation, though intangible, wields remarkable power to shape perceptions and influence our offline realities. But can this crafted identity coexist with our authentic self, or does the digital character slowly take precedence? The dance between the virtual persona and the real individual is a complex yet fascinating exploration of modern identity. As tech-savvy individuals, we're tasked with the challenge of maintaining authenticity in a space that often rewards superficiality. Understanding this dynamic reveals much about human behavior, urging us to be more mindful of the personas we project and the impacts they may have on our psyche. In this ever-evolving digital landscape, finding balance becomes not just a personal journey, but a universal quest for harmony between the digital and the tangible.

Crafting a Digital Identity

Building a digital identity is akin to sculpting a statue, starting with a rough block of marble and chipping away to reveal something distinct and personal. In the digital world, your identity isn't just shaped by static details like name or location—it evolves with every post, every interaction, and every piece of content you consume or create.

In today's hyper-connected landscape, deliberately crafting an online persona has become almost essential. What we choose to share and how we present ourselves can influence how others perceive us, both personally and professionally. This isn't about creating a fictional self. Instead, it's about emphasizing certain aspects of your personality and experiences to highlight who you are—or who you aspire to be—within the fluid, dynamic environment of the web.

Platforms like social media, blogs, and personal websites are tools that offer a canvas for constructing this identity. Each post and image, each response or share, contributes to your digital narrative. These elements build the story others read about you online, and as communicative creatures, we naturally gravitate towards narratives. How much control and intention we exert over these narratives directly influences our public and private lives.

Importantly, the crafting of a digital identity also involves understanding the audience. Who are you speaking to, and what is the message you intend to convey? This isn't just about strategic sharing but about authenticity matched with audience expectations. There's an art to being true to oneself while being attuned to the digital pulse, the ebb and flow of online culture and trends.

The authenticity paradox plays a crucial role here. On one hand, showing vulnerability and genuine emotion can strengthen connections and trust with others online. On the other, oversharing can lead to privacy breaches or unintended consequences. Finding this balance is a delicate dance, requiring introspection and a clear understanding of one's boundaries.

The risks and rewards of a well-crafted digital identity are unmatched. While it can lead to numerous opportunities, from professional advancements to personal growth, there's a shadow side that demands careful navigation. Missteps can result in misunderstandings or even reputational harm, showing that although digital identities can be fluid, they can also become entangled with real-world consequences.

Despite the risks, there's an unmistakable magic in the ability to reinvent oneself digitally. It offers a space for self-exploration and self-expression, allowing individuals to explore facets of their personality they might not express in face-to-face settings. Whether it's exploring new communities, joining niche interest groups, or launching creative projects, the digital domain is a playground for identity exploration.

The narrative of self isn't monolithic. Just as people play different roles in life—be it as a parent, friend, or colleague—so too can digital identities be multifaceted. This compartmentalization can aid in addressing the dissonance between who we are offline and who we might become online, navigating the tension between genuine expression and performative identity.

Digital identity craft also intersects with issues of privacy and data ownership. When you build a digital persona, you inadvertently weave a tapestry of data, leaving footprints that can outlast the immediate context. This posits questions not just about how you represent yourself, but how much of yourself is visible—and to whom. As digital citizens, understanding the landscape of privacy is intrinsic to mastering one's identity.

Central to managing a digital identity is the ongoing process of self-evaluation. Are the values you champion online reflective of your offline beliefs? Is the persona you project elevating your true self or masking it? Regular reflection ensures that your digital presence remains aligned with who you genuinely are, beyond the screen.

Looking forward, the evolution of the digital world introduces new opportunities for crafting identities. Technologies like virtual reality or augmented reality offer immersive experiences where traditional boundaries blur even further. In these spaces, identity can be molded in previously unimaginable ways, transcending the current limits of text and imagery-based platforms. Yet, they also challenge us to think deeply about the very essence of self when digital possibilities are endless.

Ultimately, while the tools and platforms may evolve, the core of crafting a digital identity remains rooted in human desires for connection, expression, and meaning. Embracing this process with intentionality and mindfulness allows us not only to navigate these digital spaces effectively but thrive within them. In doing so, we can illuminate the path of authenticity, even in the ever-shifting sands of the digital landscape.

Balancing Virtual and Real Selves

In a world where our virtual presence often rivals our physical one, finding a balance between our online identities and who we are in real life has become an imperative task. The advent of digital technology has allowed us to construct, modify, and present our personas in a myriad of ways. This flexibility, while empowering, can also complicate our understanding of self. How do we navigate these dual realms without losing our authentic selves?

Our virtual and real selves intersect in ways that can lead to enriching hybrid identities. Online, we can experiment with aspects of our identity, pushing boundaries and exploring different facets of ourselves in spaces that may feel safer than physical ones. This exploration can be liberating, offering a platform for self-expression that might be limited in the real world due to social norms or personal inhibitions. But the question remains: does our digital self mirror our true nature, or does it create a new narrative that only partly reflects who we really are?

Social media platforms and digital communities encourage us to maintain an "editable" self. In these spaces, one can curate their identity meticulously. It's akin to being the director of one's own personal documentary, deciding what scenes should be shown to the world. While this curation allows for a controlled expression of self, it can also lead to a dissonance between the ideal and the real. This gap between the personas we craft online and the people we are offline can contribute to a sense of unease, as if we are actors constantly shifting between roles.

Disconnecting from the digital realm can often feel like an insurmountable task, yet it's crucial for grounding ourselves in reality. By stepping away from screens and digital notifications, we create space for introspection and genuine interaction. This isn't about shunning technology but about finding moments of solitude where our thoughts are untethered by the expectation of online engagement. We need these intervals to recalibrate and ensure our values align across both spheres of existence.

The digital landscape offers numerous benefits, such as the ability to connect with others across the globe, access vast information resources, and participate in movements advocating for significant change. However, it also presents challenges in maintaining emotional authenticity. The instant gratification of a retweet or like fosters a feedback loop that equates online validation with self-worth, potentially overshadowing intrinsic sources of confidence and happiness.

To strike a balance, one must cultivate a level of self-awareness that recognizes the influences and pressures typical of digital interactions. This involves questioning whether our online behaviors and representations are truly reflective of our inner selves or if they are constructed performances that cater to external expectations. By being mindful of these distinctions, we can appreciate the freedom our digital personas provide without becoming beholden to them.

One approach to reconciling our digital and real identities is through thoughtful self-reflection and dialogue. Engaging in open conversations with trusted friends or family can illuminate discrepancies between how we present ourselves online and who we are away from keyboards and screens. Such exchanges can reveal unconscious patterns and open the door to more authentic self-presentation across mediums.

Moreover, understanding the constructed nature of online personas can arm us against the comparison trap—the tendency to measure ourselves against the carefully curated images of others. Realizing that everyone is portraying a part, rather than the entirety, of their life can free us from unrealistic standards and reinforce the perspective that our self-worth transcends digital affirmations.

Maintaining this equilibrium necessitates strategies that integrate both realms into a cohesive sense of self. Setting boundaries is essential; having digital-free zones or times can help create an environment where physical interactions take precedence. Practicing digital minimalism, intentionally choosing how we engage with technology, empowers us to focus on meaningful interactions and content that contribute positively to our sense of identity.

In essence, achieving harmony between our virtual and real selves isn't about compartmentalizing these different facets of identity but finding a seamless integration that honors both. The digital world should enhance our understanding and experience of self, acting as a mirror that reflects our core values and aspirations rather than distorting them. Within this balance lies freedom—the freedom to be grounded in who we are, both online and offline, and to engage authentically with the world around us.

Chapter 3: Connectivity and Community

In the digital age, connectivity isn't just a feature of technology; it's the lifeblood of modern community. We live in an era where relationships extend beyond physical borders, creating networks that defy geographical limitations. This blending of the tangible and virtual fosters a new kind of community, grounded in shared interests and instant communication rather than proximity alone. It's fascinating to see how individuals band together online, using social platforms to forge meaningful connections and exchange ideas. Yet, as we dive deeper into the dynamics of these digital communities, we uncover both opportunities for greater understanding and empathy, and challenges such as echo chambers and polarization. The ability to build connections across diverse groups broadens perspectives, but it's our responsibility to navigate these virtual landscapes wisely, ensuring they enrich human experience rather than diminish it.

Building Online Relationships

In the vibrant tapestry of our digital age, online relationships stand as a remarkable phenomenon, reshaping how individuals connect and interact. As each of us navigates the murky waters of our online lives, we're prompted to question the essence of these virtual connections. Are they as genuine as face-to-face interactions, or do they represent a mere shadow of true human connection? It's intriguing how technology offers both intimacy and distance in the same breath, compelling us to scrutinize the intricate dance of building and maintaining relationships online.

Consider a time when letters took days, even weeks, to traverse continents, linking distant hearts through carefully crafted words. Today, a message zips across the globe instantaneously, erasing the boundaries of time and space. This instant connection paves the way for relationships that aren't confined by geography. Friendships blossom between individuals who might never have crossed paths in the physical world. Online forums, social media, and gaming communities serve as fertile grounds for such connections, where shared interests lay the foundation for enduring bonds.

Yet, the virtual realm has its nuances. Tone and context, once easily interpreted through gestures or vocal inflections, can become muddled in text-based communication. Emojis and gifs attempt to fill the void, but they lack the depth of a subtle smile or a concerned glance. Understanding these limitations is crucial in fostering meaningful online relationships. The savvy online communicator learns to read between the lines and decipher the underlying emotions behind a screen's shield, unlocking the potential for deep, genuine connections.

The allure of anonymity can also be a double-edged sword. It offers a playground for self-exploration and expression, allowing individuals to share thoughts and pieces of their lives they might otherwise keep hidden. This can foster a sense of safety, emboldening some to open up and connect on a deeper level. For others, it tempts them to construct facades, making it challenging to discern authenticity. The anonymity that encourages vulnerability also necessitates a cautious approach, reminding us that trust must still be earned and authenticity sought.

In navigating online relationships, empathy emerges as a vital skill. Being attuned to the subtle cues embedded in digital interactions shows that distance doesn't have to dampen understanding. A heartfelt response to an online friend's troubles, or a well-timed message of support, can transcend screens, creating a bridge of compassion. The shared human experience doesn't lose its essence purely because the medium has changed. The adept navigator of online spaces knows that empathy builds sturdy connections, offering digital solace in times of need.

Social media platforms, with their sprawling networks, present another dimension of these relationships. While they provide unparalleled opportunities for connection, they also present unique challenges. The visibility of relationships on these platforms can lead to comparisons, breeding envy or dissatisfaction. Likes and comments, while often innocuous, can become a measure of self-worth, affecting how individuals perceive their online friendships. Being mindful of these tendencies helps keep the focus on the quality of connections rather than their perceived popularity.

For all its challenges, the digital realm offers opportunities for community-building that were previously unimaginable. Niche interest groups transcend local limitations, allowing individuals with rare passions to unite. These communities can be incredibly supportive, offering a sense of belonging to those who might otherwise feel isolated. Whether it's a group of artists sharing their creations or a support network for a rare health condition, these connections exemplify the positive potential of online relationships.

Technology wields the power to bring global communities closer, yet it's upon us to ensure these interactions contribute positively to our lives. Setting intentions in how we connect can help steer online relationships toward enrichment rather than disillusionment. By balancing our digital and real-world interactions, we're better equipped to foster connections that truly resonate, blending the convenience of technology with the depth of human touch.

In conclusion, building online relationships is an evolving art. It demands awareness, empathy, and a keen understanding of the digital context. As we continue navigating the intricate world of connectivity and community, these relationships will undoubtedly reshape our social landscapes. By embracing both their potential and their pitfalls, we can harness the digital world to forge deeper, more meaningful human connections, thus enhancing the rich tapestry of our lives.

The Dynamics of Digital Communities

As we delve deeper into the digital age, the nature of community itself seems to undergo a metamorphosis. What defines a community in a world where borders are pixelated lines on a screen, and connection doesn't require physical proximity? Digital communities aren't bound by geography or time; they're forged in spaces where shared interests and passions converge, creating vast networks of intertwined, often global relationships.

At the heart of digital communities lies the notion of belonging. Humans have always sought out others who are like-minded, who share values, interests, or goals. This hasn't changed with the advent of digital communities; if anything, it has intensified. The internet gives people the ability to find and connect with others who share their niche interests or peculiar pursuits. Whether it's a subreddit dedicated to medieval literature or a Facebook group for drone enthusiasts, these spaces foster a sense of belonging and identity.

However, digital communities are not a simple continuation of the physical ones. Their dynamics are complex, structured by algorithms that sometimes favor engagement over genuine interaction. Studies suggest that digital communities can be both inclusive and exclusive at the same time. The very factors that draw people together in these communities—common interests and passions—can also create echo chambers where dissenting voices are blurred, leading to polarization and sometimes, toxicity.

In many ways, the strength of digital communities is their diversity. Members can hail from different backgrounds, cultures, and countries, each bringing a unique perspective to the table. This creates opportunities for rich dialogues and the cross-pollination of ideas. But with diversity comes the challenge of communication without the nuances of face-to-face interaction, leading to misinterpretations and conflicts.

One of the fascinating aspects of digital communities is their fluidity. Unlike traditional communities, which often form around consistent and relatively static factors like location or social status, digital communities can evolve rapidly. A new technology or pop culture trend can give rise to a community overnight, just as easily as an old community can dissolve into the streams of digital history.

The governance of these communities varies widely. Some platforms tech companies moderate strictly, setting rules to maintain decorum and respect. Others operate on a self-regulated basis, relying on community leaders or moderators to keep order. This spectrum of governance and autonomy can define the community's culture, shaping whether it is seen as a safe and supportive space or something more akin to the Wild West.

The roles individuals take on within digital communities can also transform. People often start as lurkers, passively observing the interactions within the group before choosing to engage. As they become more comfortable, they might start contributing, developing respect and establishing authority. In some cases, individuals become influencers or leaders within these communities, helping guide the direction and ethos of the group.

But what happens when digital communities cross into real life? Increasingly, we're seeing physical meetups and events spring from online interactions, blurring the lines between digital and physical networking. These gatherings strengthen ties and can lead to collaborations and initiatives that digital dialogue alone might struggle to achieve.

The therapeutic potential of digital communities can't be overlooked either. For many, particularly those geographically isolated or otherwise marginalized, these spaces offer solace and support. Finding others who share similar struggles or experiences can be life-changing, reducing feelings of loneliness and providing a platform for sharing and healing.

Yet, with all the potential benefits, there's a pressing need for vigilance. While digital communities can be nurturing, they can just as easily harbor threats. Cyberbullying, misinformation, and manipulation are ever-present risks, requiring community members to be discerning and critical of the content they consume and contribute.

In effect, digital communities are the modern campfire around which people gather. But unlike traditional campfires that dim as the wood gets consumed, these digital fires burn on electric energy and human passion, providing light and warmth in the vast dark cosmos of cyberspace.

Adapting to the dynamics of digital communities requires agility and openness to new ways of connecting. It means recognizing both the promise and the perilous possibilities inherent in these spaces. It entails accepting that digital communities are neither inherently good nor bad, but rather a reflection of the nature and intent of their participants.

Ultimately, digital communities shape and are shaped by their members. They are living organisms, growing and adapting to the digital landscape around them. As we journey forward in the digital realm, how we engage with these communities will play a crucial role in defining not just our digital interactions but our broader societal fabric.

As the boundaries of community continue to expand beyond our immediate physical surroundings, the power to create meaningful, positive change rests in collective efforts. It's a reminder that whether online or off, community starts with us. Each post, each interaction molds the digital tapestry we weave every day.

Chapter 4: The Psychology of Social Media

Navigating the labyrinth of social media isn't just about mastering platforms; it's about understanding the psychological currents that draw us deeper. These online spaces tap into our primal desires for connection, approval, and self-expression, creating a landscape where every "like" and share feels like a validation of our worth. Emotions ebb and flow with each notification, shaping perceptions and self-esteem in ways society is only beginning to comprehend. Yet, in this swirling digital matrix, the allure lies not just in the content we consume but also in how it reflects and amplifies our identity, urging us towards a continual cycle of engagement. The psychology of social media is a testament to its double-edged potential—empowering, yet demanding our vigilance in navigating its emotional tides.

The Allure of Likes and Shares

In the labyrinth of social media, few elements capture human fascination quite like the seemingly innocuous "likes" and "shares." These small digital tokens have revolutionized how we interact with one another, subtly influencing our behaviors and identities in profound ways. To understand their magnetic pull, we must delve into the psychological mechanisms at play with each tap of the thumbs-up or the forward icon. They're more than just metrics; they're symbols of acceptance, validation, and connection in the digital age.

Have you ever wondered why a simple notification from Instagram or Facebook can briefly brighten your day? These platforms tap into one of humanity's most basic social needs: the need for belonging. Humans are social creatures, hardwired to seek connection and approval from their peers. The designers of social media know this intimately and have crafted these platforms to offer an almost instantaneous form of gratification through likes and shares. When someone likes our post, it triggers a dopamine hit—the brain's natural reward chemical—which reinforces our behavior and encourages us to engage further.

This source of validation isn't just about vanity or self-promotion. Beneath the surface, it reflects our innate drive to be seen, heard, and appreciated by others. People post pictures, thoughts, or achievements and, when acknowledged by their networks, feel a sense of inclusion. It's not unlike receiving a compliment in face-to-face interactions. Social media amplifies this, giving us an audience that stretches far beyond our immediate social circles.

While the immediate gratification of a digital thumbs-up is clear, the implications for self-esteem and identity are far-reaching. Many people curate their online personas heavily to optimize for more likes and shares, carefully analyzing what content gains the most traction. This phenomenon can lead to a distorted sense of self, where personal value is measured by digital interactions rather than authentic self-assessment. It becomes easy for individuals to lose sight of their intrinsic worth, measuring it instead by social media metrics.

What about the influence of likes and shares on behavior? The digital badge of popularity impacts how we act, even sparking changes in what we value and the discussions we engage in. This can create a feedback loop where the most liked and shared content steers societal focus. In this context, social media becomes a powerful tool for shaping both personal and collective narratives.

The commercial world keenly understands this. Organizations and brands leverage likes and shares to foster engagement, creating viral marketing strategies that encourage users to spread content on their behalf. Influencers, born from the social media revolution, rely heavily on this economy of approval. They craft content aimed at maximizing engagement, blurring the line between personal expression and advertising.

At the community level, likes and shares also have the power to unite. Communities coalesce around popular content, sharing similar interests and values. When someone shares an article, meme, or video, they invite others into their world, perhaps hoping to spark a conversation or cement a shared belief. Likes act as a nod of agreement, a small yet powerful acknowledgment that one isn't alone in their views or tastes.

However, the allure of likes and shares isn't all positive. The compulsion to receive digital validation can lead to anxiety, depression, or stress when those notifications don't materialize as often as hoped. For some, the drive for approval can become obsessive, leading to an unhealthy cycle of overuse as they seek reassurance and digital acceptance. It can create a social hierarchy dictated by digital popularity, enhancing feelings of inadequacy and exclusion for those at the lower end.

This dynamic shifts when likes and shares become less frequent, highlighting another critical aspect of social media psychology: the fear of missing out (FOMO). Users fear that if they don't remain constantly active, continuously contributing to their digital identities, they'll fall behind, not only missing out on interactions but on life experiences themselves. The quest for likes becomes a treadmill, encouraging ever more significant engagement with social platforms.

In light of this, understanding our own motivations for chasing likes and shares can be incredibly empowering. Recognizing the emotional boosters and detractors social media offers allows individuals to consciously decide how they want to interact with these platforms. By fostering a healthy relationship with social media, one can enjoy the benefits of connectivity and community without falling prey to the pitfalls of excessive influence and reliance.

Ultimately, it's about finding balance—an equilibrium between using likes and shares as tools for positive engagement while maintaining a grounded sense of self-worth that doesn't rely on digital currency. Embracing authenticity over perfection and genuine connection over mere numbers can lead to more fulfilling digital experiences. In a world connected by screens, remembering the humanity behind each tap or swipe is essential to navigating the psychological landscape of social media with intention and mindfulness.

Emotional Responses to Online Engagement

In the vast expanse of digital landscapes, social media has emerged as a dominant force that significantly influences our emotional lives. What makes an online platform more than just a collection of pixels and code is its capacity to evoke a complex tapestry of emotions that can fluctuate wildly from one moment to the next. This kaleidoscope of feelings—ranging from joy, validation, and connectedness to anxiety, envy, and loneliness—plays a crucial role in shaping the user experience. As we explore emotional responses to online engagement, we uncover layers of psychological processes that go beyond surface-level perceptions.

The initial draw to social media usually stems from its promise of connection. At its core, the allure lies in the human need for interaction. Social platforms provide the stage where bonds are forged and exchanged through comments, likes, and shares. Each notification acts as a pulse, reinforcing the notion that someone out there cares. It's an affirmative nod that speaks to our deeply ingrained social nature. But while these interactions can foster a sense of belonging, they can also spark a quest for validation that isn't always fulfilled, leading to what some term "social media anxiety."

Consider a typical scenario: a user uploads a post expecting a flurry of likes and comments. If the engagement falls short, feelings of disappointment or inadequacy may emerge. This "like" economy, where digital affirmations translate into emotional currency, can amplify feelings of envy and self-doubt. Such experiences suggest that as much as social media networks offer connection, they also simulate a form of competition. Observing others' curated lives can create unrealistic expectations and comparisons that are oftentimes detrimental to mental health.

Yet, it's not all doom and gloom. The emotional diversity encompassed within online engagement often propels users towards growth and self-awareness. For instance, witnessing a friend's success or resilience can inspire motivation and ambition. Happiness shared through milestone posts can evoke joy that transcends screens, reminding us of the collective human experience that binds us all. Conversely, sharing personal struggles and receiving support can foster a sense of community and empathy, allowing for emotional relief in a supportive virtual setting.

One intriguing facet of emotional responses to online engagement is the phenomenon of emotional contagion. This concept refers to the idea that emotions can spread through virtual networks much like they do in physical spaces. A friend's post expressing sadness can invoke empathy, leading others to mirror these emotions or offer comforting words. While contagious joy can uplift, contagious negativity can cast shadows over collective online experiences. Recognizing emotional contagion can serve as a pivotal step for users to consciously influence their digital environments.

The psychological underpinnings that dictate our reactions to these online interactions are complex. Brain chemistry plays a substantial role, with dopamine—the neurotransmitter associated with pleasure—often at the center. The variable rewards offered by unpredictable likes and comments release dopamine in the brain, fostering a cycle of seeking and reward that can border on the addictive. This quest for neurological delight explains why many users find themselves returning to these platforms, chasing the next wave of digital recognition.

As digital interactions have become ubiquitous, the role of empathy mustn't be underestimated. Understanding another's emotional state through online cues can be more challenging than reading physical gestures or vocal tones. Emojis and typing styles serve as new emotional signifiers, but they can sometimes lead to misunderstandings or exaggerated interpretations. To navigate these digital nuances requires not only emotional intelligence but also a willingness to communicate transparently and openly.

Despite its virtual nature, the digital world has real-world implications. Emotional responses to online engagement have the power to impact personal relationships, self-esteem, and even productivity. A study might show that people invest vast amounts of emotional energy into maintaining their online persona and fostering virtual relationships. And while these engagements can be fulfilling, a balance must be struck to ensure they don't overshadow real-world responsibilities and connections.

For many, the solution to navigating emotional responses online lies in mindfulness and intentional engagement. This means being aware of emotional triggers and actively managing one's time and interactions on social media platforms. Setting boundaries, such as designated "tech-free" times or using apps designed to monitor and limit usage, can help maintain emotional well-being. Encouragingly, there is a growing trend towards digital detoxing, which emphasizes the need to unplug and reconnect with the physical world for emotional recalibration.

Moreover, just as individuals are adapting, so too are platforms. Algorithms are increasingly incorporating features that aim to promote healthier online experiences by prioritizing meaningful interactions over mindless scrolling. These changes reflect an evolving understanding of social media's psychological impact, highlighting the industry's responsibility to foster environments that support users' mental health.

Ultimately, understanding emotional responses to online engagement requires both introspection and adaptation. As users, we play an active role in shaping our experiences and mastering the digital balance. By cultivating empathy, practicing mindfulness, and exercising critical thinking, we can harness the potential of social media without falling prey to its pitfalls. As technology continues to evolve, our ability to navigate these spaces with emotional intelligence will be crucial, leading us toward a future where digital and emotional health coexist harmoniously.

Chapter 5: Privacy in the Public Eye

As we navigate the complexities of our digital existence, privacy's place in the public eye feels more precarious than ever. In a world where personal data streams across countless platforms, the line between private and public is nearly nonexistent. Individuals willingly share glimpses of their lives, often unaware of the extended digital footprints they leave behind. The act of data sharing holds profound implications, subtly shaping our behaviors and decisions while simultaneously being scrutinized by algorithms and eyes we might never see. Amidst this, we must confront the profound realization that our digital activities are embedded in a web of surveillance that transforms anonymity into an artifact of the past. By understanding these dynamics, we can become architects of our own privacy, fostering an awareness that drives deliberate choices about how we present ourselves in this interconnected reality. Here lies the challenge—and the empowerment—in reclaiming our narrative within the digital cacophony, making way for a future where privacy isn't just a relic, but a right worth preserving.

Navigating Digital Privacy Concerns

In our digital age, privacy has transcended its traditional boundaries. No longer confined to the tangible aspects of one's life, it now encompasses the vast and intricate mesh of the internet. As the digital landscape evolves, so too does the way we perceive and engage with privacy. It's become a complex tapestry that we're all trying to navigate, understanding the implications of each thread and how it weaves into our daily lives.

At the heart of these developments is the staggering amount of personal data being generated every second. Whether through social media updates, online purchases, or even the innocuous browsing of a favorite blog, our actions leave a digital footprint that can be traced, analyzed, and potentially exploited. For the tech-savvy individuals, this isn't just an abstract concept. It's a tangible concern that requires vigilance and a keen understanding of digital barriers.

The first step in addressing digital privacy concerns begins with awareness. Understanding the breadth of information that is collected about us is crucial. Take, for instance, the ubiquitous smartphone. It knows where we are, what we're doing, and with whom. Many apps request access to various device features, often more than is necessary for their functionality. This collected data can paint a detailed picture of a person's life, making consent and informed decision-making more important than ever. Recognizing this, individuals must cultivate a habit of regularly reviewing privacy settings and permissions across their devices and platforms.

Privacy in the digital realm is not just about personal vigilance; it extends to the regulations and laws that govern it. Varied regions have implemented measures like the General Data Protection Regulation (GDPR) in Europe, which aims to protect user data and give individuals more control over their personal information. While such regulations are a step in the right direction, they also highlight inconsistencies on a global scale, opening up discussions on how these varying laws intersect and what they mean for users worldwide.

However, legislation can only do so much. As the digital world becomes more decentralized, individuals must also take responsibility for their own privacy. This includes being discerning about what they share online and who can access that information. There's an inherent tension between the benefits of connectivity and the risk of exposure. Social media platforms, for instance, thrive on user data to enhance connectivity and personalization, yet this very same data can be leveraged to infringe upon personal privacy. Users must weigh these trade-offs, often making decisions that have no clear right or wrong answers.

One approach to fostering better privacy practices is through education and digital literacy. By empowering individuals with knowledge about how their data is used and the potential vulnerabilities, they can make informed choices. This leads to another layer of digital citizenship — understanding not just the technological aspects, but also the ethical and psychological implications of one's online behavior.

There are also technological solutions that can assist in safeguarding privacy. Tools like encrypted messaging apps, virtual private networks (VPNs), and two-factor authentication offer additional layers of protection. However, these are not foolproof, and users must remain skeptical, continually seeking to understand new technologies and potential threats.

Innovation doesn't pause, and with each new device or application, privacy concerns are reborn in a new guise. In this tech-driven world, staying static isn't an option. We must persistently adapt, staying informed about emerging trends and potential risks. Such proactive behavior not only ensures one's own security but fosters a culture of awareness that can ripple through communities.

Moreover, navigating digital privacy concerns is also a matter of introspection. Each individual has different thresholds for privacy and risk. Some willingly embrace the trade-offs for greater personalization and convenience, while others remain more reserved. Engaging in open dialogues about these perspectives can lead to a richer understanding of privacy's evolving role in our lives and how we might collectively navigate these challenges.

As we look to the future, the intersection of technology and privacy demands our attention and creativity. Solutions may involve a blend of individual effort, technological innovation, and societal shifts towards transparency and accountability. Building a digital environment that respects privacy without stifling progress is akin to crafting a piece of art — it requires vision, patience, and collaboration.

Ultimately, the journey of navigating digital privacy is one that calls for a recalibration of our understanding, not just of technology but of ourselves. How we choose to engage with these concerns is reflective of our values and aspirations. As we traverse this digital world, a mindful approach can illuminate the path to a future where privacy and progress thrive in harmony.

Implications of Data Sharing

In a world where our lives unfold across digital screens, the privacy of personal information is more important than ever. Data sharing has become a ubiquitous part of our digital interactions, and its implications are profound. With the tap of a finger, individuals broadcast details about themselves — from preferences and routines to intimate moments — across platforms. But beneath the surface, each data point we share contributes to an ever-expanding tapestry of information that's not just about us, but also about our collective human experience.

The allure of sharing data stems from a desire to connect and be understood. Platforms promise customization, targeting content and advertisements to fit our tastes perfectly. It feels personal, almost serendipitous, when they get it right. Yet, behind this veneer of personalization lies a complex system of data harvesting and analysis. Companies gather immense amounts of data to refine algorithms, predicting behaviors with uncanny accuracy. While this might enhance user experience, it raises pressing questions about how much control we're surrendering. Are we truly aware of what we're trading for convenience?

One can't ignore the power dynamics embedded in data sharing. Major corporations possess capabilities to influence consumer behavior, most of it powered by our shared data. These firms hold vast repositories of human preference, often operating without full transparency or regulatory oversight. This imbalance can lead to a form of digital manipulation, where users are subtly guided to make decisions aligned with the interests of these powerful enterprises. Are we becoming passive players in a game orchestrated by invisible hands?

Moreover, data sharing has implications for personal identity and autonomy. Every piece of data adds to a digital representation of who we are. But is this digital self an accurate reflection of our true selves, or merely a distorted caricature shaped by algorithms? With each shared detail, we risk commodifying our identities, reducing the rich tapestry of human experience to entries in a database. This transformation raises significant questions about authenticity and the value of our digital personas.

On a broader scale, the societal implications of data sharing extend to issues of security and surveillance. Governments and law enforcement agencies leverage data to maintain social order, arguing that increased surveillance ensures safety and security. But at what cost? The extensive reach of digital surveillance challenges fundamental freedoms, potentially infringing on privacy rights. In seeking to preserve security, we must carefully balance our collective safety with individual liberty.

Additionally, there's the issue of consent. As data flows between platforms and companies, understanding where our information travels becomes nearly impossible. Often, terms of service agreements are so lengthy and convoluted that users may not fully understand what they're agreeing to. This lack of clarity undermines informed consent, leaving consumers vulnerable to unexpected uses of their data. Are we unwitting participants in a grand experiment without full knowledge of its parameters?

However, it's worth noting that not all data sharing is intrinsically negative. In healthcare, for instance, shared data can drive innovation, leading to breakthroughs in treatments and disease prevention. The collective power of shared information can pave the way for advancements that benefit humanity. But even in benevolent applications, it's crucial to implement safeguards to protect individuals' rights and privacy, ensuring that the benefits are distributed equitably.

Despite these challenges, data sharing isn't inherently detrimental. Humanity thrives when knowledge is pooled and experiences are shared. This sharing can stimulate creativity, foster innovation, and nurture empathy among diverse groups. The key lies in navigating this new digital landscape with awareness, ensuring that the mechanisms of data sharing are equitable and transparent.

Ultimately, understanding the implications of data sharing requires us to examine the interplay between technology and human behavior. Our interconnected digital world requires a nuanced approach, recognizing the dual role of technology as both a tool for empowerment and a mechanism of control. As we stand at the crossroads of opportunity and risk, the choices we make today will shape the future of our digital selves and societies.

By rethinking how we share data, we can envision a world where digital interactions enhance rather than encroach upon personal freedoms. It's an opportunity to craft a paradigm where data is used responsibly, fostering a digital realm that enriches human life without compromising the essence of privacy. Such a future demands intentional action, where technology serves humanity's best interests rather than its basest instincts.

Chapter 6: Information Overload

In today's hyperconnected world, we're constantly bombarded by a deluge of information, data, and digital noise that can overwhelm even the most tech-savvy individuals. Our brains, evolved for slower-paced, linear information processing, now grapple with a ceaseless flood of emails, notifications, and content updates, leading to cognitive overload. This incessant stream not only affects our ability to focus but can also obscure our decision-making processes, leaving us feeling scattered and anxious. Yet, amidst the chaos, there's an opportunity to cultivate digital mindfulness. By harnessing technology purposefully and establishing clear boundaries, we can transform this overwhelming tide into a manageable flow that enriches rather than exhausts our mental faculties. Embracing these strategies, we reclaim control over our digital lives, fostering a sense of balance and clarity in an era defined by perpetual connectivity.

Managing Digital Content Consumption

The digital age has ushered in an era characterized by an abundance of information. This phenomenon, known as information overload, represents a challenge and a marvel of our time. Digital content consumption management emerges as a critical skill as we navigate vast oceans of data streaming across our screens.

In today's hyper-connected world, individuals are bombarded by an endless barrage of articles, updates, notifications, and digital media. With each click and swipe, we absorb an overwhelming mix of useful insights, entertaining diversions, and distracting noise. The real challenge lies not just in consuming content but in discerning what merits our attention.

The Consequences of Overconsumption

Much like mindlessly consuming unhealthy food, unchecked digital content consumption can lead to mental and cognitive distress. Our attention is a finite resource, stretched thin by competing digital demands. Overconsumption often results in decreased productivity, increased stress levels, and a fragmented state of mind.

The psychological loading from digital content isn't just about the volume but about the nature of the information, too. When we attempt to process too many incoming streams at once, we invoke a continuous partial attention state. In this scenario, we respond to constant signals from digital devices without deeply engaging with any of them, impairing our cognitive capacity and robbing us of truly satisfying insights.

Navigating the Digital Deluge

How do we tackle this challenge and manage our digital diets adeptly? The first step lies in adopting a mindful approach to content consumption. Just as one might thoughtfully choose a meal for nutrition, we can curate our digital intake. This starts with establishing priorities—identifying the content that aligns with our goals, values, and intellectual curiosity.

Carefully selecting sources and platforms that foster meaningful engagement encourages a healthier digital ecosystem.

Another technique is to build intentional 'digital downtime' into daily routines, similar to fasting periods. These intervals serve as scheduled breaks from the relentless stream of news and notifications, allowing our minds a chance to refresh and refocus. Additionally, creating boundaries around start and end dates for digital interactions ensures we allocate time to digest information properly without constantly being 'on'.

Embracing Technology as an Ally

Ironically, technology itself offers tools and strategies for its own management. Applications and browser extensions can help filter, organize, and limit exposure to unnecessary content. These tools can serve as guards, helping to sift through the noise and present what's most relevant or valuable to our defined purpose.

Technological solutions aren't just about filtering but involve orchestration of how we engage with digital content. Features such as read-later lists, customizable alerts, and app usage analytics empower users to make informed decisions about their digital interactions. Embracing data thoughtfully can guide users to construct a balanced digital life, leveraging technology as an ally rather than a threat.

The Role of Introspection and Self-awareness

Despite the effectiveness of various strategies and tools, self-awareness remains a critical component in managing digital content consumption. A keen understanding of one's habits, triggers, and preferences can illuminate pathways towards healthier digital experiences.

Through introspection, individuals can recognize what draws their attention most and why, often revealing deeper insights into personal motivations and habits. This understanding can further refine one's content consumption strategy, steering it towards truly enriching digital interactions and away from more addictive, less fulfilling distractions.

In embracing a self-aware digital lifestyle, mindful interactions replace reactive consumption, fostering contentment and clarity instead of disorientation and stress. It's about creating a personal and impactful relationship with technology where the user control remains paramount.

The Future of Content Consumption

As the digital landscape evolves, new forms of media and content delivery will inevitably emerge. Anticipating this future implies recognizing that today's strategies may need adaptation to suit tomorrow's challenges. The commitment to lifelong learning in digital literacy becomes essential, as ongoing education equips individuals to handle novel digital phenomena with agility and poise.

Moreover, as the paradigm shifts towards more immersive media experiences, like virtual reality and augmented reality, the ways we consume content will change. These new dimensions pose exciting possibilities and also bring forth new considerations in managing content consumption. The skill will lie in recognizing immersive experiences' potential for both insightful engagement and possible detachment from reality.

Ultimately, managing digital content consumption is an evolving journey, one grounded in balance, intention, and introspection. By cultivating these practices, we can transform the overwhelming influx of information from a source of distraction into a wellspring of knowledge and fulfillment. It's about reclaiming agency in our digital interactions and embracing a future where technology amplifies the human experience, rather than diminishes it.

Strategies to Combat Online Fatigue

In a world where screens dominate our attention and every ping or notification demands immediate acknowledgment, it's no surprise that online fatigue has emerged as a prevalent modern malaise. Information overload isn't just about the sheer quantity of content we wade through every day but the consequent exhaustion that comes from trying to keep up. The constant inundation of data leaves many feeling mentally drained, leading to a sense of fatigue that permeates through their personal and professional lives.

The first step in combating this fatigue is acknowledging its existence. Recognizing that you feel overwhelmed by the nonstop digital demand is not a sign of weakness but a natural response to an unnatural situation. It's crucial to set boundaries, ensuring that online lives don't encroach too heavily on our offline ones. By creating a clear delineation of time spent online and offline, individuals can begin to reclaim control over their attention and energy.

One effective strategy is establishing a digital diet. Just as with food consumption, it's not only about reducing intake but also focusing on quality. Curate online experiences to prioritize content that enriches and informs rather than overwhelms. Consider unfollowing accounts that add little value or introduce undue stress, and subscribe to content that's uplifting or intellectually stimulating instead.

A practical approach involves the intentional design of digital environments. Reducing visual clutter on devices can significantly lessen stress. Declutter app screens, organize folders, and set aside specific times to check emails and messages. The use of toolbars or extensions that limit the number of open tabs can narrow focus and discourage multitasking, which is often less productive than we believe.

Time management becomes an ally in this battle. Implementing time-blocking techniques, where specific hours are set aside for digital tasks, can help regulate consumption. Designating screen-free times, particularly before bed, can enhance sleep quality and reduce fatigue, providing the brain with much-needed respite from continuous stimulation.

But hand-in-hand with these structural changes comes the need for a shift in mindset. Knowing when to disconnect is vital. Embrace the philosophy that it's okay not to be constantly available. Turning off notifications for non-essential applications reduces pressure to respond immediately, allowing space for more profound focus and creativity.

Mindfulness practices can also play a pivotal role. Introducing short moments of meditation or guided breathing exercises into daily routines can help reset mental focus and alleviate digital stress. Techniques such as "digital fasts," where one deliberately refrains from online engagement for set periods, can offer a stronger sense of control and myriad psychological benefits.

Finding balance often requires external support. Engage in conversations with others who may be experiencing the same fatigue. Sharing strategies and experiences can foster community and mutual support, creating a network where individuals feel less isolated in their experiences and more empowered to make meaningful changes.

Employers can also contribute by adopting policies that respect digital boundaries. Encouraging regular breaks, delineating expectations around after-hours communication, and promoting a culture that values mental health can all contribute to reducing online fatigue. Companies that recognize the impact of information overload and actively work to minimize it can lead to happier, more productive employees.

Ultimately, combating online fatigue is about reclaiming a sense of agency in a digital world that never sleeps. By implementing strategic changes both personally and within wider communities, there's an opportunity to cultivate a more balanced relationship with technology. This balance not only serves the individual by refreshing their mind and spirit but also enhances one's overall quality of life, allowing for more meaningful offline experiences.

While technology has reshaped nearly every facet of existence, it's vital to remember that humans hold the power to define its role in their lives. By consciously choosing how and when to engage with the digital world, there's potential to not just survive in this age of information overload but to thrive. The key is consistent, deliberate action, and a willingness to adapt strategies to fit one's lifestyle.

As tempting as it might be to seek definitive answers in a constantly evolving digital landscape, acceptance of a flexible, adaptive approach is often most effective. The dynamics of online fatigue are complex, and the strategies that work today may need refinement tomorrow. Yet, through awareness and choice, individuals can navigate this terrain with greater ease, resilience, and a sense of fulfillment. This balance is not just a necessity; it is a gateway to a more enriched life amid the digital torrent.

Chapter 7: The Impact on Mental Health

The digital world is reshaping the contours of our mental landscapes, unleashing both empowering connections and formidable challenges. Technological advances have fostered communities that transcend geographical barriers, yet they also introduce a unique set of stressors—a complex interplay of overexposure to information, social comparison, and digital fatigue. As we navigate this relentless stream of connectivity, understanding its repercussions on mental health becomes critical. We find ourselves constantly tethered to a digital presence, which, despite its undeniable benefits, has the potential to erode our mental well-being if left unchecked. Each notification, ping, and alert can heighten anxiety or, paradoxically, numb it through an addictive loop of reactions and validations. It's crucial, then, that we develop robust coping mechanisms, ones that encourage a balanced engagement with technology, focusing on nurturing mental resilience amid the digital din. Embracing these strategies not only harnesses the positives of our online interactions but also provides a bulwark against the psychological pitfalls endemic to our increasingly digital lives.

Exploring the Digital Stressors

As we navigate through the vibrant yet intricate maze of our modern digital environment, it becomes increasingly crucial to acknowledge the stressors that accompany this journey. Technology, with its myriad of benefits, doesn't just amplify convenience; it can also amplify pressure. Our tech-savvy audience is no stranger to the rapidly evolving digital terrain, yet the psychological weight of constant connectivity often remains understated.

At the heart of this pressure is the relentless stream of information that bombards users every waking hour. From breaking news alerts to social media notifications, there's a continual barrage that demands attention. This phenomenon, often termed as "information overload," saturates our mental bandwidth and contributes significantly to stress levels. It's akin to trying to drink from a fire hose—overwhelming and unsustainable. This fast-paced influx of information can lead to decision fatigue, making once-simple choices feel daunting.

Part of the challenge lies in the way information is packaged and presented. Algorithms, designed to capture and hold our attention, sometimes prioritize sensational over substantive content. The result is a digital space that thrives on keeping us perpetually engaged, instigating a cycle of anticipation and anxiety about staying updated. For tech-savvy individuals, this can create an invisible pressure to remain constantly 'in the know', lest they fall behind in discussions and debates that rapidly evolve online.

Moreover, the omnipresence of social media platforms compounds this stress by fostering a culture of comparison. These digital realms often present curated realities, where users showcase idealized versions of their lives. This disparity between one's online portrayal and actual life circumstances can cause feelings of inadequacy. Constantly measuring oneself against others can drain emotional resources and lead to diminished self-esteem.

Another stressor stems from the expectation of immediate responses in digital communication. The blinking cursor of a messaging app is a constant reminder of our hyper-connected world, where reply times are often measured in seconds. This expectation can create an environment rife with anxiety, particularly for those who struggle with setting boundaries in their digital interactions. The pressure to maintain conversational momentum contributes to a feeling of being perpetually 'on call', which can erode mental tranquility over time.

The landscape is further complicated by the intrusion of work-related communications into personal time, largely facilitated by our mobile devices. The blurring boundaries between work and personal life lead to what is often referred to as "techno-stress." This perpetual tethering to work-related responsibilities impacts personal relationships and exacerbates feelings of burnout.

Data security fears also loom large as a significant digital stressor. With increasing instances of cyber theft and breaches, users are often caught in a cycle of worry about their personal information's vulnerability. This can manifest as anxiety regarding the security of online financial transactions or the broader implications of identity theft. The complexity of safeguarding digital data is a stressor, as it forces individuals to become vigilant custodians of their own online safety, an additional cognitive burden they may be ill-prepared to bear.

In addition to these stressors, there's a growing concern about the physical impacts of digital immersion. Screen time has escalated dramatically, leading to lifestyle repercussions such as disrupted sleep patterns and reduced physical activity. The effects of blue light on sleep cycles are well-documented, and lack of rest can compound psychological stress.

Amid this digital flux, cognitive dissonance often emerges, particularly concerning ethical implications. Users grapple with their personal values against the often contradictory practices of tech giants. This internal conflict adds another layer to the digital stress spectrum, as individuals are forced to navigate their beliefs within a digital domain that frequently operates under different moral compasses.

All is not bleak within the digital realm; recognizing these stressors is the first step towards mitigating their impact. The tech-savvy individual is uniquely positioned to leverage technology to foster stress-reducing habits. Awareness and education about digital wellness practices can serve as a beacon, guiding users towards healthier tech relationships. Wielding the power of technology to practice mindfulness, for instance, could offer therapeutic benefits against the very stressors it often creates.

In the face of these digital challenges, fortifying mental health becomes an essential endeavor. Understanding the landscape of digital stressors not only equips individuals with the knowledge to better navigate their online worlds but also inspires a more harmonious coexistence with technology. As we delve deeper into exploring coping mechanisms in the following section, one's capacity to flourish within the digital ecosystem will prove to be not just beneficial, but necessary for thriving in our interconnected era.

Coping Mechanisms in an Online World

In an era where digital exposure is inevitable, understanding how to cope with the incessant stream of information becomes crucial to maintaining mental health. The internet, while a wonderful vortex of creativity and connection, can also be an overwhelming source of stress. For tech-savvy individuals, who navigate this realm with ease, it's easy to dismiss the underlying toll it takes on our mental well-being. Here, we explore pragmatic strategies that empower individuals not just to survive but to thrive in this digitized environment.

First and foremost, acknowledging the root of digital stress is pivotal. Many individuals experience what psychologists term "continuous partial attention". This phenomenon refers to the constant, ever-present part of our awareness being taken up by digital alerts and notifications. It's a silent, creeping stressor. To counterbalance this, it's essential to create moments where you detach from screens entirely. Scheduling regular digital detoxes—times when you consciously decide to unplug—can rejuvenate your mind and redirect your focus towards real-world interactions and self-reflection.

Furthermore, setting boundaries within our digital lives isn't just beneficial; it's necessary. The internet has erased the boundaries between work and personal time. To restore balance, individuals can establish strict tech-free zones or hours at home. This simple act is transformative, carving out space for more mindful pursuits like reading or engaging in hobbies that don't involve screens. By delineating when and where technology is used, individuals reclaim control over their time and attention.

Yet, it's not always about abstaining from digital connections. Sometimes, it's about changing how we interact with them. For instance, cultivating a mindful relationship with social media can reduce the anxiety associated with endless scrolling. This involves being intentional about the content you consume and the people you interact with. Curating your digital milieu to reflect positivity and encouragement fosters a digital environment that supports rather than detracts from mental health.

Incorporating mindfulness into digital habits can also be quite effective. Techniques such as mindful browsing allow individuals to bring awareness to their digital interactions. Instead of mechanically swiping through feeds, taking a moment to ask why you're consuming certain content or how it makes you feel can significantly shift your online habits. Integrating mindfulness apps that remind you to pause and breathe amidst your browsing can serve as checkpoints for mental clarity.

Building online communities focused on support rather than comparison is another powerful tool. These communities can offer a refuge where digital citizens share experiences, support one another, and create a sense of belonging. When utilized properly, these platforms can enhance mental stability by reinforcing that no one is alone in their struggles with digital anxiety. Opting into forums and groups that prioritize constructive dialogue creates a buffer against isolation, turning virtual spaces into havens of optimism and creativity.

Lest we forget, the value of offline support should not be underestimated. While technology connects people globally, it is our offline relationships and experiences that ground us. Attending offline meetups of interest groups or participating in events that bring digital acquaintances together in the real world strengthens bonds and satisfies our innate need for human connection. Physical interaction has immeasurable power to counteract the feelings of loneliness that can arise from an overly digital existence.

The therapeutic advantages of traditional practices like journaling also offer solace. Encouraging individuals to write down their feelings about their online interactions can lead to heightened self-awareness and emotional processing. This practice bridges the gap between one's online and offline worlds, providing clarity and perspective on how the virtual world influences one's emotional landscape.

Ultimately, integrating these coping mechanisms won't eliminate digital stress entirely, but they'll surely soften its impact. Having an arsenal of strategies tailored to suit one's lifestyle ensures that the digital world remains a tool rather than a tyrant. For tech-savvy individuals, the journey to maintaining mental health in an online world is about balance and choice—choosing when to connect and when to disconnect, when to engage and when to retreat. In this dance between the digital and the real, we find not only coping strategies but pathways to resilience and growth.

Chapter 8: Digital Dependency

In our hyper-connected world, technology has become both a boon and a bane, weaving itself into the very fabric of our daily existence. As we explore the phenomenon of digital dependency, it's evident that the constant access to information, entertainment, and social interaction brings about a paradox: while the digital world offers convenience and immediate gratification, it often leads to an insidious erosion of our ability to disconnect and experience life in its unfiltered form. This dependency on technology for emotional and cognitive sustenance raises critical questions about self-identity and autonomy, pressing us to confront our growing reliance on screens. For tech-savvy individuals, this awareness is a call to action, urging us to cultivate a mindfulness that embraces technology as a tool, rather than a tether. By finding a harmonious balance in our digital consumption, we empower ourselves to harness the best of both the virtual and tangible worlds, striving not just for a life of connectivity, but one of meaningful connections.

Recognizing Technology Addiction

Technology has embedded itself into nearly every facet of our lives, so much so that its omnipresence often feels normal. But when does this digital embrace transform into something more consuming, even addictive? Recognizing technology addiction isn't straightforward. Much like traditional forms of addiction, it sneaks up subtly, often cloaked in the guise of productivity or social connection. The constant ping of notifications, the irresistible lure of endless scrolling, or the dopamine rush from 'likes'—all contribute to a cycle that's hard to break.

Imagine a day starting not with the sun's rays but with the glowing screen of a smartphone. Eyes barely open and yet already consumed by the digital world. This scenario is not unusual. The fine line between healthy engagement and addiction lies within our behaviors and their consequences. Are we using technology as a tool, or are we its tool? This question requires reflection. Small triggers—such as anxiety when separated from a device—can reveal underlying dependencies.

The design of digital platforms plays a significant role in fostering addiction. Algorithms are meticulously crafted to capture attention and keep us engaged. Ever wondered why it's so hard to put down the smartphone or close that browser tab? It's by design. We are bombarded with stimuli designed to be as engaging as possible, and our psychological responses are increasingly fine-tuned to these stimuli. Behavioral scientists have identified components like variable reward schedules or social validation that keep users returning for more.

Consider the social validation loop and its impact on technology addiction. The notifications from social media platforms promise a reward—likes, comments, or shares—that can be intoxicating. There's a powerful allure in the idea that a digital audience values your thoughts and content. But this kind of validation can morph into a relentless craving. The feedback loop fosters an environment where self-worth is increasingly tied to virtual approval, propelling users to engage more frequently and intensely.

For some, the impact of technology addiction manifests visibly in neglected responsibilities and strained relationships. People's lives are shaped—sometimes dominated—by their digital interactions, often at the expense of physical presence. When virtual interactions consistently overshadow real-life engagements, the balance tips unfavorably. This can lead to a disconnection from the actual world around us, as we become more engrossed in our screens.

Yet, recognizing technology addiction doesn't only apply to extreme cases. It also involves acknowledging the more subtle shifts in behavior. Perhaps it's the constant need to check notifications or feeling compelled to capture every moment for online sharing. These behaviors might seem benign but can signal deeper issues of dependency. When one feels a sense of panic at the thought of their phone being out of reach, it's a stark indicator of potential addiction.

Interestingly, age plays a role in how technology addiction is experienced and recognized. Younger generations, often termed digital natives, might not perceive their continuous digital engagement as problematic. For them, constant connectivity is a norm rather than an anomaly. Meanwhile, older users might experience heightened self-awareness about their digital consumption and make more conscious attempts to regulate it.

Another component to consider is the interplay between anxiety and technology use. Studies have shown that individuals may use their devices as a way to escape feelings of loneliness or social anxiety. Paradoxically, excessive use can exacerbate these feelings, reducing face-to-face social skills and increasing a sense of isolation. The very tool used to diminish discomfort can amplify it, creating a vicious cycle.

Academic research supports the notion that technology addiction can alter brain patterns similarly to substance use disorders. The flood of dopamine from digital interactions creates pleasure, leading individuals to repeat behaviors despite negative consequences. Over time, this can reshape neural pathways, making it increasingly difficult to diminish the compulsion to engage with technology.

Understanding the cultural context is also necessary for recognizing this addiction. In many communities, the expectation to be constantly available and responsive has become the norm. This is especially true in professional settings where the boundary between work and personal time is increasingly blurred. The demand for instantaneous communication can trap individuals in a continuous cycle of connectivity, increasing the difficulty of setting boundaries.

The path to recognizing technology addiction often begins with introspection. It's about assessing whether digital behaviors align with one's values and if they're enhancing or detracting from life's meaningful aspects. It involves questioning whether technology serves a purpose or is simply filling a void. This awareness can be the first step toward modifying habits and regaining control.

Furthermore, it's vital to cultivate environments where open dialogue about technology use is encouraged without judgment. Sharing experiences and challenges can demystify addiction, making it easier to identify and address. Support networks, whether online or in person, can provide guidance and encouragement for those seeking a healthier relationship with their digital world.

In conclusion, recognizing technology addiction is as much about self-awareness as understanding the external forces at play. It demands honest reflection on how technology impacts our lives and relationships. By identifying the signs and understanding the underlying mechanisms, individuals can begin to reclaim agency over their digital interactions. Engaging with technology consciously and purposefully can transform the digital landscape from a potential source of addiction into a realm of opportunity and growth.

Finding Balance in Digital Use

Our digital age offers immense possibilities. From keeping us connected across continents to providing instant information, technology has seeped into almost every aspect of our lives. However, this infiltration, while advantageous, also beckons us to pause and ponder the personal balance between virtual interaction and our physical reality.

Imagine waking up to the gentle chime of your alarm — your ever-present smartphone. It's a mundane start but sets the tone for a day awash in technology. We are habitually glued to our screens, checking notifications even before our feet touch the floor. This isn't just a morning ritual; it's a reflection of modern existence. The prevalence of technology isn't inherently damaging, but when screens replace physical interactions, an imbalance can ensue. This imbalance often leads to feelings of disconnect, despite our connectedness.

At the heart of this digital dance lies a critical question: how can we utilize technology without becoming enslaved by it? The answer, like many things, isn't prescriptive but personal. It demands a shift from mindless engagement to mindful interaction. By fostering a conscious awareness of our tech habits, we can better align our digital lives with our true selves.

Consider an evening walk. No music, no podcasts, just the rhythmic sound of your footsteps. Such moments of detachment can act as a reset button, recalibrating our senses and reinforcing our connection to the present. By deliberately carving out these pockets of tech-free time, we nourish our mental well-being. This is not to vilify technology but to acknowledge the need for boundaries. Just like any tool, technology serves us best when used intentionally.

Let's look at social media, a predominant driver of digital dependency. While a powerhouse of connectivity and communication, these platforms are often designed to retain our engagement through endless scrolling and notifications. The allure is potent but can disconnect us from the here and now. Recognizing this, some users have begun to set specific timeframes for social media interaction, freeing up mental space for other activities.

Creating physical spaces designated as tech-free, such as the dining table or bedroom, can also foster this harmony. These zones encourage conversations and moments of contemplation, enriching our daily experiences. Establishing these boundaries not only aids in reducing dependency but enriches the quality of our interactions.

Mindfulness techniques are another tool in our arsenal. Practices such as meditation can help anchor us in the present moment, offering clarity and reducing the constant urge to check our devices. This doesn't require a radical lifestyle change but rather integrating small, deliberate moments of stillness into our daily routine.

Incorporating digital detoxes into our regular schedule can further enhance this balance. These detoxes don't imply a complete disconnection but rather a strategic timeout. They allow us to step back and evaluate our digital consumption, offering fresh perspectives on how we interact with technology.

Yet, it's crucial to acknowledge that finding balance isn't a one-size-fits-all solution. Individual needs vary, and what might work for one person might not suit another. The path to balance is personal and often requires trial and error. It's about discovering what enriches our lives and what detracts from it.

There's a growing movement among tech enthusiasts and digital experts advocating not just for a reduction in screen time but for a richer utilization of it. They suggest being selective about the digital tools we use, prioritizing those that genuinely add value to our lives. This conscious curation can lead to more meaningful interactions, both online and offline.

The discourse around digital dependency also invites us to delve deeper into our collective psyche, questioning why we gravitate towards our devices. In many cases, it's an escape, a void-filler. By understanding these underlying motivations, we can address the root of our dependency and explore healthier alternatives.

Ultimately, the goal is not to abandon technology but to embrace it in a way that enhances our quality of life. By prioritizing real-world interactions and cultivating a mindful approach to digital engagement, we can foster a balanced relationship with technology. As tech-savvy individuals who constantly navigate the digital landscape, awareness and adaptability become our greatest allies.

As we move forward, embracing the balance between digital use and real-world interaction becomes crucial. It's a conscious choice, one that empowers us to dictate the terms of our technological engagement rather than being dictated by it. In this evolving narrative of digital life, each one of us holds the pen, ready to script a future that resonates with balance and intentionality.

Chapter 9: Virtual Relationships

In a world where our screens increasingly become portals to connection, the way we form and sustain relationships has morphed in profound ways. Virtual relationships bring us closer, transcending geographical barriers while challenging the very essence of intimacy. Today, bonds are forged not with physical presence but through flickering pixels and instant messages that create new norms of emotional exchange. We navigate these digital interactions with a unique set of cues and expectations, redefining trust and closeness in the process. Yet, beneath this vast web of connectivity, digital conflicts arise, from misinterpretations to the ephemeral nature of online affirmations. However, these challenges also teach resilience, fostering a growth in understanding and compassion as we learn to bridge gaps and celebrate individuality through virtual means. By embracing both the power and the pitfalls of online intimacy, we see not just a reshaping of human connections, but a testament to our ability to adapt and flourish in an ever-digital world.

Understanding Online Intimacy

The tapestry of human relationships is undergoing a transformation. In the digital era, where bytes and bits connect us, intimacy often takes a new shape. This isn't merely about the increasing frequency of text messages or video calls replacing face-to-face interactions. It goes deeper, mingling with the human psyche in remarkable ways, encouraging us to redefine what closeness means in the context of virtual space.

Consider the reach of the internet. It's stretching across towns and countries, collapsing geographical boundaries, and enabling us to encounter individuals we'd never meet otherwise. The ability to form intimate bonds with this seemingly boundless array of individuals is both a thrilling and daunting prospect. Technology enables relationships to thrive beyond physical presence, yet it also demands we learn new skills to nurture these connections.

One of the critical facets of online intimacy is how it allows us to explore new dimensions of ourselves. Our digital communications often compel us to distill our thoughts and emotions into a different language—a virtual lexicon of emojis, memes, and gifs that convey feelings in merely milliseconds. This form of expression, as ephemeral as it might seem, adds a layer of richness to interactions, forging connections that are both surprising and profound.

The anonymity afforded by the internet grants a unique form of intimacy, one where individuals may reveal their inner selves without fear of immediate judgment. Paradoxically, this anonymity can breed authenticity, as people share more openly when the everyday constraints of social anxiety are diminished. However, this also requires a heightened level of emotional intelligence, as we learn to interpret intentions and feelings without the aid of physical cues or vocal tones.

Consider how the intimacy of online relationships can often mirror traditional connections but develop at a different pace. The rapid exchange of messages can create a sense of closeness quickly, yet sustaining deep, meaningful bonds requires patience and understanding. Much like a traditional relationship, online intimacy demands investment —time, empathy, and sometimes vulnerability.

- Understanding emotional cues in text.
- Navigating the balance of public and private sharing.
- Fostering trust in a digital environment.

Each of these constitutes important elements in building intimate connections online. The speed and convenience of digital communication can often mask the need for thoughtful engagement. Online platforms create spaces that thrive on rapid exchanges, but true intimacy demands slowing down, taking the time to listen and respond with care.

Another vital aspect of understanding online intimacy lies in the realm of digital identity. In the limitless realm of virtual reality, individuals can craft and project versions of themselves that resonate with their true or aspirational selves. This freedom means that the people we meet online might present themselves in ways that are more aligned with how they see themselves, or hope to be seen, than they might in everyday physical interactions.

This varied expression of self provides fertile ground for intimacy to flourish. By interacting through avatars and profiles, we're offered a glimpse into another's curated world, allowing for unique bonds to form. Yet, forming connections based on these digital presentations also poses challenges—how do you discern what is real from what's contrived, and how much does that really matter?

There's an inspirational aspect to witnessing the blossoming of relationships in such environments. As individuals open up about their experiences, whether mundane or profound, they build networks of support that transcend traditional barriers. Communities generate their own rituals of intimacy, such as shared gaming sessions or collective storytelling, creating worlds that tighten the bonds between their members.

The implications of online intimacy stretch beyond personal experience, potentially reshaping societal understandings of relationships. The impact of these connections offers a laboratory of sorts, where experiments with human connection might forge new paths for empathy and understanding on a global scale. Despite the screens that separate us, or perhaps because of them, we're capable of building bridges of such strength that they redefine the contours of intimacy.

As we journey deeper into the digital age, there's a motivational call to action for nurturing these virtual bonds while remembering the essence of human interaction. The medium may alter, but the core of empathy, understanding, and mutual support remains unchanged. This fusion of traditional values with technological advances invites us to explore a future where virtual relationships aren't just a substitute for face-to-face interactions but a valuable addition to the human experience.

In conclusion, online intimacy is a complex tapestry woven from the threads of connectivity, anonymity, and digital identity. It challenges us, urging us to redefine what closeness looks like. But in its unique way, it also enhances our lives, broadening the scope of how we connect and communicate. While the digital landscape offers new frontiers for intimacy, it reminds us that the human heart has always had an astonishing capacity to adapt, grow, and connect, regardless of the medium.

Navigating Digital Conflicts

In the labyrinth of online interactions, conflicts are inevitable. Digital platforms, with their blend of anonymity and immediacy, often magnify misunderstandings. When communicating face-to-face, subtle body language and tonal variations guide comprehension and empathy. Yet, these elements are absent online. Words become blunt tools, sometimes cutting deeper than intended. As our relationships migrate to the digital realm, we must learn new ways to navigate these choppy waters and wrestle with the conflicts that arise.

Conflicts in virtual relationships often stem from the absence of shared physical context. In person, a smile or a nod quickly reassures someone of goodwill; online, these cues vanish. Misinterpretations become common, fueling disputes over what might have been trifles in real-life conversations. A simple punctuation mark – or lack thereof – can transform a benign message into an incendiary one, illustrating how fragile virtual communication can be. To thrive in this landscape, we must sharpen our written communication skills and practice patience, learning to read between the lines with a generous assumption of intent.

The rapid pace of digital communication doesn't help. Instant messaging apps, social media platforms, and email all demand rapid responses, which can escalate tensions. In our haste to reply, we might react rather than reflect, leading to heated exchanges that might have been avoided with a pause or a cooling-off period. Embracing the art of slow communication could be key in these instances. Deliberate responses allow for deeper reflection, reducing the impulse to respond reactively.

Anonymity on digital platforms complicates matters further. It emboldens some to express thoughts they'd typically suppress if their identities were known. This phenomenon, termed the "online disinhibition effect," can lead to more frequent and intense conflicts. The cloak of anonymity might unleash a torrent of unchecked aggression, amplifying disputes that would be otherwise restrained. Acknowledging the human on the other end of the conversation and engaging with empathy can counteract this effect, making it crucial for maintaining civility online.

Additionally, the public nature of many digital platforms adds pressure to conflict resolution. Disagreements might unfold not just between two individuals, but before an audience of friends, family, or even strangers. This shift in the conflict dynamic often intensifies emotions, as the participants may feel pressure to "win" in the eyes of their witnesses. In such scenarios, privacy settings and private message functions can prove invaluable, providing the space necessary to resolve grievances away from watchful eyes.

Resolving digital conflicts also requires a certain mindfulness about the medium itself. Each platform has its own culture, norms, and etiquettes. A comment that might be acceptable in one forum could be reprehensible in another. Understanding these nuances and adjusting one's communication style accordingly is fundamental. Educating oneself about platform-specific behaviors is not only strategic but respectful, allowing smoother navigation of potential disputes.

However, it's not enough to just understand these virtual landscapes; actively fostering digital environments that preemptively address conflict can be transformative. Encouraging open dialogues, using inclusive language, and promoting digital literacy can build communities resilient to conflict. Here, education plays a pivotal role. By equipping individuals with the tools to articulate thoughts clearly and empathetically, we reduce the chances of digital misunderstandings turning into conflicts.

It's also important to recognize the psychological tools available to us in these situations. Addressing our own cognitive biases, like the negativity bias – our predisposition to perceive messages negatively – can help stem conflicts before they begin. By consciously challenging our initial reactions and seeking clarity where uncertainty exists, we can navigate misunderstandings more adeptly.

Contrarily, digital conflicts can offer unique opportunities for growth. Navigating such disputes can build resilience and hone communication skills applicable across contexts, both online and offline. Learning to resolve disagreements in this arena can strengthen not only virtual relationships but also interpersonal skills more broadly. This reframing of conflicts as opportunities rather than threats can inspire a more optimistic approach to digital interactions.

As we continue to explore these digital landscapes, it becomes apparent that conflicts, while inevitable, can be managed and even turned into constructive experiences. With the right tools and mindset, the virtual world offers as much potential for harmonious relationships as the real world. Ultimately, understanding these dynamics enhances our appreciation of digital life and fortifies our ability to maintain healthy connections amidst the chaos of online interaction.

Chapter 10: Educating for a Digital Future

As technology continues to weave into the fabric of everyday life, the question of how to educate for a digital future has never been more pressing. This chapter explores the necessity of equipping individuals with the skills to navigate and thrive in an ever-evolving tech landscape. It's about more than just understanding how to use the latest gizmos or platforms; it requires a deeper grasp of digital literacy, where critical thinking and ethical considerations join hands. By cultivating these competencies, we prepare future generations to not only consume but also question and innovate responsibly. The interplay between education and technology can broaden minds, reshape societal norms, and inspire a future where humanity and technology coexist harmoniously. The potential impact on the human psyche is vast and holds the promise of profound new ways of thinking and interacting — a future brimming with possibility if nurtured thoughtfully and inclusively.

Teaching Digital Literacy

As we immerse ourselves in the sprawling digital universe, the importance of teaching digital literacy can't be overstated. At its core, digital literacy transcends the mere ability to use technology; it involves understanding how to navigate the intricate web of digital information while critically evaluating the content we consume. With the proliferation of digital platforms, this skill is not just critical for survival in today's technology-saturated world, but also for thriving and contributing meaningfully.

Digital literacy is more than just knowing how to "click." It's about making informed decisions when faced with an overwhelming amount of information. In an age where data is abundant and integrity is frequently questioned, fostering the ability to discern fact from fiction is pivotal. This skill is often likened to having a well-tuned compass that can guide us through the often stormy seas of digital information.

The landscape of digital literacy extends to understanding the ethical dimensions of digital interactions. We must teach not only the technical use of platforms but also the implications of our digital footprint and the responsibilities that accompany it. Ethical digital literacy raises questions: How do we ensure our online interactions reflect our offline values? How do we protect our privacy while engaging in digital expression? Addressing these questions forms a significant part of a comprehensive digital literacy education.

Moreover, digital literacy isn't a one-size-fits-all concept. It must evolve along with the technological innovations that shape our daily lives. Educators and technologists are challenged to stay ahead of the curve— constantly adapting curricula to include AI's impact or the role of augmented reality in our communications. The fluid nature of technology means that what we teach must remain flexible, being just as much about equipping individuals to learn independently in an ever-changing digital landscape as it is about imparting specific skills.

In teaching digital literacy, an often-overlooked aspect is inclusivity. There is a digital divide that runs along socio-economic lines, and bridging this gap is crucial. Digital literacy programs must be accessible to everyone, regardless of background, age, or geographic location. Equal access ensures that no segment of society is left out of the digital transformation shaping every facet of our existence.

Practical implementation of digital literacy education starts with the foundational ability to interpret digital content. This involves a shift from passive content consumption to active and critical engagement. Learners should be encouraged to ask, "Who created this content? What is its purpose? Does it align with known facts?" This analytical approach fosters a deeper understanding and prevents the spread of misinformation.

We must also cultivate operational skills such as data management and cybersecurity awareness. The value of knowing how to protect oneself online has never been more pronounced. Cybersecurity literacy is akin to being street-smart in the digital age, understanding both the vulnerabilities and defenses available in an interconnected world.

Perhaps one of the most inspiring aspects of teaching digital literacy is the empowerment it brings. It enables people to participate in democratic processes, engage in meaningful global dialogues, and make informed consumer choices. In a sense, digital literacy is the gateway to full participation in modern society.

Lorem ipsum dolor sit amet, consectetur adipiscing elit. Maecenas tempus lacus non nibh iaculis, at accumsan mauris lobortis. Nulla sit amet lacus eu lectus convallis elementum. Ut ac tempor velit, in porttitor dui. Donec sit amet quam nec lorem pharetra tincidunt non eu neque.

Integration of interdisciplinary approaches is key in teaching digital literacy. While technology is its backbone, it must interweave elements of psychology, sociology, and ethics to provide a holistic educational experience. Understanding how technology affects our cognitive processes, for instance, is as crucial as mastering the latest software.

The role of educators extends beyond the classroom walls, especially in the context of digital literacy. Parents and guardians play a crucial role in fostering these skills from an early age. Encouraging healthy digital habits, setting screen time limits, and discussing online experiences broadens the educational environment, turning every interaction into a learning opportunity.

The future beckons with technologies we can hardly imagine today. Preparing for this uncertainty is a daunting yet exciting challenge. Digital literacy education prepares individuals not only to adapt to change but to influence it, steering the digital ship towards a future that mirrors societal values while encouraging innovation.

Finally, we are reminded that teaching digital literacy is a continual process. It's not a destination, but rather a journey. As technology evolves, so too must our understanding and our teaching methodologies. Preparing for a digital future means accepting that learning never truly ends, and that curiosity and adaptability are perhaps the two most vital skills of all.

Preparing for the Evolving Tech Landscape

The world isn't just watching the tech landscape change; it's an active participant in its daily evolution. Technology's relentless pace defines our era, shaping behaviors, communities, even individual identities. For those with a deep affinity for the digital realm, the prospects are both thrilling and daunting. This perpetual flux demands not just awareness but preparedness—a readiness to adapt, learn, and grow in sync with the emergent technologies that come our way.

Education becomes crucial in this context. It's no longer about learning mere operational skills but embracing a holistic understanding of technology's vast and often unpredictable impact on human nature. To truly prepare for the evolving tech landscape, we must foster an environment that values curiosity, continuous learning, and a willingness to challenge preconceived notions.

In modern learning environments, educators and learners alike must work together to build a flexible framework that accommodates rapid changes. This isn't about designing rigid curriculums that become obsolete by the time they're implemented. Instead, it's about creating adaptable skill sets that encourage critical thinking, problem-solving, and an understanding of technology's broader effects on society.

Adaptability also means embracing the unforeseen. The digital realm is characterized by its ability to defy expectations. A seemingly small technological advancement can lead to significant societal shifts. This unpredictability requires embracing uncertainty and developing a mindset that can pivot rather than resist when innovations occur.

Furthermore, an appreciation for cross-disciplinary learning is essential. The borders between technology and other fields are becoming increasingly blurred. Artists leverage AI to create new forms of expression, while doctors use VR for surgical training. Engineers might collaborate with psychologists to design user-centric digital tools. Such hybrid skills highlight the necessity of an interdisciplinary approach to educational practices.

The evolving tech landscape also questions what it means to be a digital citizen. How do individuals manage their identities and personal interactions amid rampant technological advancements? Ethical considerations, privacy, and accountability stand at the forefront, urging an alignment between individual actions and societal values. This requires more than technical know-how; it calls for a deep-seated understanding of how technology intertwines with ethics and human behavior.

In addition, the digital future will likely challenge our traditional concepts of work. Automation, AI, and machine learning are reshaping workplaces. Jobs once considered untouchable by machines are now under threat of replacement or transformation. This shift demands an ongoing commitment to lifelong learning, where up-skilling and re-skilling become crucial to staying relevant.

Technology also brings unprecedented opportunities for active learning and innovation. Today's learners have access to a plethora of online resources, tutorials, and forums that transcend geographical and economic barriers. The capacity to learn from global experts, participate in virtual communities, and engage in collaborative projects opens up new horizons and fosters a more connected and democratically empowered society.

Preparing for the future isn't just about handling present technological tools but envisioning what lies ahead. Fostering foresight is essential. What could AI mean for socio-economic structures? How might virtual reality alter interpersonal communication? What roles will digital realities play in shaping narratives and histories? These questions require deductive reasoning and imagination, tools that education must equip for navigation through the vast, unchartered digital seas.

Finally, it's imperative that we do not lose sight of our humanity in the face of technological advancement. True preparedness in an evolving tech landscape involves fostering self-awareness, empathy, and emotional intelligence. These human-centric skills will determine how effectively technology serves us in a meaningful way, without replacing the essence that makes us human.

As much as technology represents our collective progress, so too must our education systems reflect a nuanced understanding of its impacts. Only by preparing the mind and spirit for continual growth, curiosity, and resilience can we hope to thrive in this ever-shifting digital future and uncover the profound possibilities it holds for all of us.

Chapter 11: The Future of Self in a Digital Today

As we stand on the cusp of even more profound digital transformation, the notion of self is poised for dramatic evolution. Our digital landscapes, expanding rapidly, are not just tools but extensions of ourselves. They reflect our values, shape our behaviors, and challenge our identities. Living in this digital today means continually adapting as technology reshapes our personal and collective lives. We must ask: who are we when our identities can shift as swiftly as software updates, and how do we preserve the core of our humanity amidst such fluidity? While the influx of new technologies offers unprecedented possibilities, it also demands a critical examination of their influence on our sense of self. Embracing these changes with both curiosity and caution will be key to navigating the uncertain terrain ahead, empowering us to craft a future that aligns with both our digital and human aspirations.

Predicting Digital Evolution

In an age where digital landscapes shift faster than the sand in a storm, attempting to predict the trajectory of our digital evolution seems like a daunting task. Yet, understanding where we're heading is crucial for shaping how we adapt and thrive in a technology-driven world. This involves not only technological advancements but an insight into human behavior and societal changes driven by these advancements.

The relationship between humans and technology is symbiotic, constantly morphing and evolving. What's particularly fascinating about this dance is how our digital identities are forged and adjusted, not only by external technological shifts but by our internal psyche. In this context, predicting digital evolution doesn't just mean foreseeing the next gadget or app; it's about anticipating how our perceptions, interactions, and inner selves will transform as we integrate deeper into digital realms.

Historically, technology has surged through predictable stages: introduction, adoption, saturation, and eventual obsolescence or transformation. Take the printing press or the telephone, for example. Both started as technological marvels and evolved into commonplace necessities, shaping society's core foundations in their wake. The same model seemingly applies to digital technologies, yet there are numerous unique nuances.

What complicates the prediction of digital evolution is the internet's unparalleled capacity for interconnection, which rapidly accelerates change. By facilitating an almost instantaneous exchange of ideas and innovations, the internet creates an environment where adaptation must occur at an accelerated pace. This speed leads to widespread and diverse impacts that can be both empowering and overwhelming.

These impacts manifest in our daily lives as altered communication forms, from brief text messages replacing long conversations to emojis and GIFs acting as universal languages. Each development subtly molds our self-perception and social strategies, mirroring both our conscious and unconscious responses to technology's presence.

Thus, predicting digital evolution involves predicting the shifts in how we express and understand ourselves and each other. Consider how artificial intelligence and augmented reality expand possibilities: AI reshaping industries and societies with capabilities ranging from automating tasks to personalizing human experiences, while augmented reality blurs the lines between the tangible and digital worlds.

There's no denying that such technologies offer incredible opportunities, yet they also pose profound questions about identity and ethics. As we hand over tasks and responsibilities to machines, what does this mean for our agency? If AR creates entirely new environments for engagement, how do we keep our grip on what's real and what's imaginative?

One can't overlook the ethical lens through which this evolution must be viewed. Digital evolution isn't merely about optimizing convenience or enhancing efficiency; it's about ensuring ethical standards that respect human dignity, privacy, and rights. The exponential growth of facial recognition technologies, for example, calls into question issues of surveillance and consent that society must address before it reaches a point of no return.

Moreover, the social implications of digital evolution are profound. How we view personal success, engage in relationship-building, and even form community life will continue to be recalibrated in response to technological innovations. As roles and expectations shift, so will mental health landscapes. Greater connection can lead to increased isolation or empowerment, depending on individual and collective approaches to managing this evolution.

In foresight, those steering technological development hold significant accountability. Innovators and policymakers must ally with ethicists, psychologists, and educators to ensure that technology elevates human potential rather than hinders it. Preparing future generations for what's next means ingraining digital literacy, not merely in terms of proficiency with devices but in a deeper understanding of the intertwined relationship between humanity and its creations.

The future of the self in a digital world hinges on our current acknowledgment and understanding of these dynamics. Predicting digital evolution requires an anticipation of shifting landscapes in technology and an empathetic comprehension of humanity's role within this change. Our capacity to adapt rests on maintaining a balance between embracing innovation and fostering a meaningful existence in both virtual and physical realms.

As we navigate through the uncertainties of tomorrow, we must remain both inquisitive and grounded. While technology propels us forward, it should not alienate us from our essence. Therefore, predicting digital evolution is about understanding possibilities and crafting a vision that harmonizes advancement with the core tenets of what it means to be human.

In closing, it is not only our foresight that shapes the future of technology but our commitment to utilizing this foresight to build a world that's more introspective and inclusive. Our digital journey lies in the gaze of imagination, waiting to be eagerly and cautiously sculpted.

Adapting to Technological Changes

In the rapidly shifting landscape of today's digital world, the ability to adapt to technological changes defines not only our personal growth but also influences our collective evolution as a society. The cascade of advancements in digital technology presents both daunting challenges and exciting opportunities, urging us to rethink the nature of our existence as inherently intertwined with technology. To thrive amidst this digital transformation, we must cultivate a mindset that embraces flexibility and foresight.

Digital technology's relentless pace of innovation requires agility in thought and action. As new devices, platforms, and digital services emerge, they continuously reshape the way we interact with the world. From the adoption of smartphones to the integration of artificial intelligence in everyday tasks, these technologies demand that we remain open to learning and re-learning skills that are pivotal in a tech-centered world. It's no longer enough to merely keep up; adaptability has become a core competency.

Consider the profound impact of virtual reality and augmented reality in redefining experiential possibilities. These technologies transform not only entertainment and education but also professional fields such as healthcare and engineering. For instance, surgeons now hone their skills using VR simulations, offering practice in a risk-free environment. However, this potential also entails a responsibility to critically evaluate how such tools alter our perceptions and interactions.

As we embrace technological changes, fostering digital literacy becomes paramount. It's not just about understanding how to use technology, but comprehending its implications on our values, ethics, and behaviors. The ability to discern credible information from a sea of digital content, and the critical thinking skills needed to navigate complex digital infrastructures, are competencies that shape our engagement with technology and with each other.

Moreover, the digital realm demands a reevaluation of the social contracts that underpin our interactions. As technology alters communication dynamics and power structures, we find new ways of relating to each other—often transcending geographical boundaries. However, it also presents challenges in maintaining privacy and authenticity. Adapting to these changes means constantly recalibrating our norms and expectations.

In this age of digital metamorphosis, businesses too must pivot and adapt to survive and prosper. Organizations that lead with a vision aligned with technological innovation often find themselves at the forefront. They leverage data analytics, machine learning, and automation to enhance efficiency and deepen customer engagement. However, it is vital for these organizations to balance innovation with ethical considerations, ensuring that technology benefits society at large without exacerbating inequalities.

Navigating technological change is not a solitary endeavor. It involves a collaborative effort across disciplines, cultures, and generations. It calls for conversations and collaborations that can bridge gaps in understanding and creativity. By fostering inclusive dialogues, we can ensure that technology reflects diverse perspectives and serves a broader spectrum of needs.

While the excitement of innovation is palpable, it is also necessary to acknowledge the anxiety that accompanies constant change. As individuals, we may grapple with feelings of obsolescence or challenge our sense of competence. Here, the human penchant for resilience comes to play. While technology evolves, human adaptability—our ability to learn, unlearn, and relearn—remains a timeless asset. It's about finding our stride amidst the flux, perhaps even discovering dormant talents in the process.

Ultimately, adapting to technological changes transcends acquiring new skills or embracing latest devices. It's about nurturing a mindset that finds comfort in discomfort—a willingness to explore the uncharted and embrace the unknown. It's about understanding that change is not a threat but an opportunity to improve the human experience and expand our potential.

In embracing these changes, we pave the way for a future where technology augments our capabilities while honoring our humanity. With each digital leap, we chart a course that beckons innovation in ideals and actions, igniting a collective mission to harness technology for the greater good. How we respond to this mission will define not just the future of self in a digital today, but the essence of humanity itself.

Chapter 12: Ethical Considerations in Digital Spaces

In the rapidly evolving digital landscape, one can't overlook the ethical dilemmas that often accompany technological advancement. These digital spaces, though rich with potential, are fraught with challenges that test our moral compass. From social media platforms teeming with misinformation to the anonymity that emboldens online harassment, each click and interaction carry a weight of responsibility. The key is fostering a culture of responsible digital behavior. Ethical considerations demand a conscious effort towards transparency, accountability, and respect for others while navigating the virtual world, ensuring that technology enhances rather than erodes our shared humanity. As tech-savvy individuals, we are called to examine not just what technology can do, but what it should do, shaping a digital future that mirrors our deepest values and highest aspirations.

Examining Online Ethics

As we delve into the intricacies of online ethics within digital spaces, it's essential to recognize how the digital realm challenges our conventional understanding of ethical behavior. The cloak of anonymity and the vast spaces in which individuals interact provide fertile ground for ethical dilemmas that might remain unencountered in face-to-face interactions. In the digital world, the lines between right and wrong, permissible and impermissible, often blur, requiring a new, nuanced understanding of moral responsibility.

People have always been social creatures, guided by societal norms and ethical codes. However, the internet's vast and mostly unrestricted playground presents scenarios we've never before encountered at such a scale. The sense of connection and community can sometimes overshadow the need for ethical vigilance. Consider social media platforms, where the race for likes and shares might tempt users to disseminate half-truths or overly sensational content. The consequent spread of misinformation isn't just a breach of trust; it reflects a broader ethical challenge in digital interactions.

In online spaces, ethical decisions aren't always just about overt harm. The impact of passivity, such as ignoring online bullying or failing to report harmful content, poses significant ethical questions. Users find themselves amidst situations where the act of doing nothing might also hold moral weight. This realization invites introspection about personal ethics and what it means to actively participate in the digital domain. Are we merely spectators, or do we have a responsibility to shape a digital community grounded in moral principles?

Transparency and honesty, mainstays of any ethical framework, face unprecedented tests online. Consider the rise of deepfakes and digitally manipulated content, which can distort reality in ways previously imagined only in science fiction. These technologies challenge the basic trust users place in the information they consume. How can one discern between what's authentic and what's fabricated when the lines are so deftly blurred? As digital citizens, the need for critical thinking and media literacy becomes paramount, reshaping our ethical compass amidst this dynamic landscape.

Amidst these challenges, we must also ponder the responsibility of those who control digital platforms. The algorithms that govern what content surfaces can amplify divisive information or perpetuate viral misinformation. Here lies a pivotal question: Do these tech giants hold ethical obligations to prioritize accuracy over advertisement revenue? The role of corporate ethics in ensuring a healthy digital ecosystem is increasingly crucial and often debated. If companies act predominantly in their own interests, where does that leave the individual?

Moreover, the responsibility extends beyond those who run platforms to the very users themselves. Ethical considerations in digital spaces beckon each individual to reflect on personal accountability. Are likes, shares, and comments mere mindless clicks, or do they echo one's values and beliefs? Encourage and promote a culture where users take a moment to evaluate the consequences of their online actions. Every interaction leaves a digital footprint, weaving into the broader tapestry that defines the online ethos.

As with any evolving field, the guiding principles of online ethics must remain flexible, adapting to new realities and technologies. This adaptability should not come at the cost of core values like respect, honesty, and kindness. Instead, they can form a steadfast foundation upon which new norms are built as innovations arise. We can draw parallels with traditional ethics and modify them to serve as a guiding beacon in this tech-centric world.

Furthermore, ethical frameworks within digital spaces are not homogenous; they vary across cultures and societies, adding another layer of complexity. The global nature of the internet brings disparate ethical norms into sometimes sharp contrast. While some practices might be acceptable in one culture, they could be perceived as unethical in another. This divergence poses a challenge yet also an opportunity for cross-cultural dialogue about universal digital ethics. We can embrace diversity and work towards a more cohesive ethical structure that respects individual differences.

The key takeaway is the need for a collective effort to forge a path toward ethical digital spaces. It necessitates participation from all stakeholders, including governments, corporations, and individual users. Educational institutions play a pivotal role in imparting digital ethics as part of broader digital literacy programs. They can equip future generations with the skills and mindset needed to navigate ethical quandaries in an increasingly connected world.

In conclusion, examining online ethics isn't just about identifying ethical transgressions; it's about advocating for a conscientious digital existence. As we continue exploring the ever-expanding digital universe, our moral compass will guide us towards healthier interactions and relationships. We must strive to cultivate an environment where ethical considerations align with technological advancement, fostering a digital world that is as morally sound as it is innovative. Only through a concerted, deliberate effort can we hope to create digital spaces that not only reflect our values but also elevate them.

Encouraging Responsible Digital Behavior

In our rapidly evolving digital world, the significance of responsible digital behavior has never been more crucial. As technology weaves itself into the fabric of our daily lives, understanding the implications of our online actions becomes a vital component of ethical engagement. Digital spaces, once simply tools of convenience, now shape human interactions and influence societal values. The challenge, therefore, lies in promoting digital behavior that respects the individual and the community without stifling innovation or creativity.

The digital age is fraught with complexities that challenge our moral compass. The anonymity offered by online interactions can tempt users to behave in ways they wouldn't in face-to-face settings. This raises a question: How do we encourage behaviors that support a thriving and constructive digital society? It begins with recognizing that ethical behavior online isn't inherently different from real-world scenarios. The rules of decency and respect remain constant, despite the medium.

Education plays a pivotal role in fostering responsible digital behavior. Schools and educators must prioritize digital literacy, equipping individuals with the tools to navigate online spaces with integrity. Knowledge about digital footprints, the permanence of shared content, and the impact of cyberbullying forms the bedrock of this education. By instilling these principles early on, we build a generation that naturally aligns with responsible digital behavior.

Moreover, it's not just about imparting technical skills; it's about teaching critical thinking and empathy. When individuals understand the emotional and psychological effects of their actions on others, they're more likely to interact responsibly. Encouraging empathy in digital communications shifts the focus from reactive behavior to thoughtful interaction, promoting an online culture grounded in understanding and respect.

Technology companies and platforms also bear a responsibility in this ethical equation. By designing user-friendly systems that prioritize user control and transparency, companies can enhance ethical interactions. Features like clear privacy settings, easy reporting of inappropriate content, and algorithms programmed to minimize harmful interactions support responsible digital engagement. This proactive design ethos can significantly impact how individuals interact within digital environments.

Social norms also play a decisive role in shaping digital behavior. Just as society collectively establishes acceptable behavior in public settings, so too must it define what is considered ethical online behavior. Community guidelines and norms within digital platforms help establish a shared understanding of unacceptable behaviors such as trolling, hate speech, and misinformation. When these are clearly communicated and evenly enforced, they contribute to a sense of collective responsibility.

Accountability is another cornerstone of responsible digital behavior. Platforms and users alike must be held accountable for their actions to maintain trust and integrity within digital spaces. For platforms, this means consistently applying policies and effectively moderating content. For individuals, it means being aware of their influence and potential repercussions on their digital community. A transparent accountability system encourages personal responsibility and deters irresponsible actions.

Cultivating responsible digital behavior also involves empowering individuals to manage their digital identities mindfully. This includes understanding the long-term implications of sharing personal information online and making informed decisions about one's digital expression. By facilitating access to better privacy tools and controls, individuals are better equipped to protect themselves and others from potential harm.

Innovative solutions can also empower users to engage responsibly in digital spaces. For instance, using technology to promote pause and reflection before sharing contentious comments or information can reduce impulsivity. Tools that encourage this kind of mindfulness can transform digital landscapes into more thoughtful and respectful environments.

Despite these efforts, it's essential to acknowledge that digital spaces will always present unique ethical challenges. As technology continues to advance at an unprecedented pace, the conversation around ethical digital behavior must remain dynamic and responsive. Regular, open discussions among developers, policymakers, and users about emerging ethics in digital spaces will ensure that the digital world evolves in a direction that benefits everyone.

In essence, encouraging responsible digital behavior requires a multifaceted approach that blends education, technological innovation, and community engagement. By fostering an environment where individuals are educated in digital ethics, equipped with the necessary tools, and supported by thoughtful community guidelines, we can cultivate a digital world that is as respectful and empathetic as possible. This is not just an aspirational goal but a necessary direction for a society increasingly intertwined with digital life, ensuring that technology enhances, rather than detracts, from the human experience.

Conclusion

As we stand at the intersection of advancing technology and human evolution, it's critical to reflect on how our digital experiences shape us. The digital landscape is no longer a separate realm; it has seamlessly woven itself into the very fabric of daily life. Our challenge, and indeed our opportunity, lies in understanding how this integration impacts our identity, relationships, and mental health, all while navigating the complexities of privacy and ethics.

In our quest for connectivity, we've crafted multiple personas—balancing our digital selves against our real-world identities. This delicate dance, juggling the curated perfection of social media with the imperfect authenticity of offline life, demands a keen awareness. We must ensure our online presence empowers rather than confines us, allowing for genuine self-expression without the shackles of digital validation.

The allure of likes, shares, and virtual acknowledgment is undeniable, often driving our behaviors and emotions. These interactions extend beyond mere exchanges; they are symbolic threads that knit together the global digital community. Yet, amid the likes and notifications, we mustn't overlook the potential for emotional turmoil. The spectrum of feelings invoked by online engagement—from euphoria to anxiety—requires intentional management. Recognizing this dynamic empowers us to forge not just meaningful connections, but also healthier interactions.

Moreover, the omnipresent connectivity continually blurs the lines between public and private. Data-sharing practices that seemed innocuous years ago now warrant rigorous scrutiny. As digital citizens, fostering a culture of privacy awareness becomes paramount to safeguarding personal information in an age where everything seems accessible. This awareness encourages more responsible behaviors and demands transparency from the big players who govern our data.

The sheer volume of information available at our fingertips, while a boon for knowledge acquisition, also has its drawbacks. Information overload can lead to decision fatigue and cognitive strain, necessitating strategies for managing digital content consumption. Filtering the vast oceans of data efficiently allows us to regain control and focus our cognitive energies on what truly matters.

With technology's ubiquity, the impact on mental health cannot be overstated. We are only beginning to understand the psychological effects of constant online engagement. From digital stressors to technology addiction, these challenges highlight the need for coping mechanisms that resonate with our experiences. Embracing a balanced approach to tech use mitigates potential harms and fosters a healthier relationship with our devices.

The relationships we cultivate online reflect the complexities of human interaction in this digital age. Virtual spaces enable us to connect deeply across distances, yet they also introduce new kinds of conflict and misinterpretation. Learning to navigate these interactions with empathy and understanding enhances our digital coexistence.

Looking ahead, educating ourselves and the next generation for a digital future is imperative. Digital literacy should encompass not only technical skills but also critical thinking, empathy, and ethical understanding. Preparing for technological shifts means embracing adaptability, ensuring we're not passive observers but active participants in shaping our tech-dominated world.

Ethical considerations in digital spaces demand urgent attention. As we delve deeper into virtual landscapes, the moral implications of our choices grow in complexity. Encouraging responsible digital behaviors ensures our actions contribute positively and benevolently to the online ecosystem, fostering environments of trust and respect.

In conclusion, embracing our digital lives with intention offers unprecedented opportunities for personal and societal growth. By cultivating awareness, adaptability, and responsibility, we elevate the quality of our digital experiences. The future, though rife with challenges, is equally brimming with promise—each byte and click a testament to our ongoing journey of digital self-discovery.

Appendix A: Appendix

As we journeyed through the realms of digital existence in this book, we unearthed various intricacies that weave technology into the fabric of our daily lives. This appendix serves as a supplementary lens, offering clarity where complexity may have lingered and expanding upon the nuanced elements woven into each chapter.

The digital world isn't just a backdrop; it's a dynamic, ever-evolving entity influencing every aspect of personal and societal behavior. In navigating these cyber landscapes, understanding becomes our compass, guiding us through a kaleidoscope of interactions, identities, and emotional landscapes.

Delving into these digital terrains reveals both the allure and the weight of online personas. As technology reshapes the way we communicate and form communities, it also molds our sense of self and belonging. The intent here isn't to dictate a path but to shine a light on possibilities, fostering a conscious awareness of our online and offline dualities. Through this comprehension, we equip ourselves to balance our virtual and real worlds with a newfound resilience.

Privacy—a facet perhaps more volatile and delicate than any other—is addressed not as an unattainable ideal but as a right to be vigilantly safeguarded. Navigating this digital labyrinth means advocating for transparency and proactive engagement, laying rest to ambiguity with informed choices.

In facing the torrents of information that surge through digital channels, strategies emerge to shield our psyche from the deluge. By practicing mindful consumption, we learn not just to endure, but to thrive amidst this ceaseless flow. Recognizing when technology transforms from a tool to a tether is a pivotal insight, encouraging us to reclaim agency over our screen-laden lives.

Lastly, as we stand on the precipice of an unpredictable digital future, we carry with us the wisdom gathered—seeds for nurturing an ethically conscious and technically literate society. With this foundation, we prepare not merely for what's to come but to shape what might be.

Through understanding, ethical reflection, and a readiness to adapt, we forge a path towards a symbiotic existence with technology, ensuring it elevates rather than diminishes our human experience.

This appendix, while a resting point, is far from an endpoint. It's an invitation to remain curious, to question, and to cultivate a deeper connection to the digital forces that animate our world, for in this dance between the virtual and the visceral, we craft the story of our time.